A Time to Speak

A Time to Speak

*Christian believers in the West
tell how they have suffered
because of their faith in Jesus*

David Waite

New Wine Press

New Wine Ministries
PO Box 17
Chichester
West Sussex
United Kingdom
PO19 2AW

Scripture quotations are taken from the following versions of the Bible:

KJV – King James Version. © Crown copyright.

NIV – The Holy Bible, New International Version. Copyright © 1973, 1978, 1984 by International Bible Society. Used by permission of Hodder and Stoughton Limited.

RSV – Revised Standard Version. Copyright © 1946, 1952 by the Division of Christian Education of the National Council of the Churches of Christ in the United States of America.

TNIV – Today's New International Version. Copyright © 2001, 2005 by International Bible Society.

ISBN 978-1-905991-34-1

Typeset by CRB Associates, Reepham, Norfolk
Cover design by CCD, www.ccdgroup.co.uk
Printed in Malta

Contents

PART 2

Foreword

by Rev. Stephen Gaukroger

The book you are about to read is about persecution. Ever since the Declaration of Human Rights was signed on 10th December 1948, human rights have been a major issue. No more so than today. Today, people of many faiths are facing persecution because of what they believe. This book is about Christians who face persecution because of their faith in Jesus Christ.

In today's secular society human rights are being challenged. No more so than for Christians who, even in Western countries like England and the United States, may not be able to practise their faith freely. Increasingly there are different ways in which society and individuals are persecuting people of faith.

This book is a wake up call because persecution has already begun and is present in these countries. The stories you will read are about real people, real situations. Their names and identities have been changed to protect them, otherwise they could face severe persecution and possibly death.

Why is this book important? It's important for all Christians to read because the people in your church, in your fellowship, in your neighbourhood may already be being persecuted because of their beliefs. You need to be able to identify with them and to help them stand firm in the face of persecution.

If you have been persecuted because of your faith in Jesus Christ, then this book is for you. It will help you understand that you are not alone, that there are others like you. If you know someone who is facing or has faced persecution themselves, it will help you understand the issues they face. Sometimes the stories have a happy ending, sometimes they remain unresolved. But this one fact remains – with Jesus Christ you can stand firm in your faith.

It is definitely *a time to speak* out and in a prophetic way let the Church be aware that these issues are coming to the people of our nations.

The first part of this book tells the stories of real people and the challenges that they have faced as a result of their faith. The second part of this book tells you what you can do in your situation and how you can help people who face persecution, both in your own country and also in the wider world.

This book has been sponsored by Open Doors which was founded by Brother Andrew in 1955. Open Doors serves persecuted Christians worldwide and exists to strengthen the Church to be a follower and advocate of Christ in the most hostile places. With over fifty years of experience, I would urge you to support this ministry as a practical outworking of your own faith.

David Waite has been associated with Open Doors since the early 1970s when he worked as a member of staff in the UK office for three and a half years. He continues to have links since leaving Open Doors to pursue other projects, and in his capacity as a writer has interviewed Brother Andrew several times over the years for various UK publications.

It is a time to speak out. It is a time for you to read, to listen, and stand up and speak.

As you read the pages of this book, may God challenge you to take personal action. The words of the Apostle Paul are as true now as when he wrote to the Corinthians, "... *have equal concern for each other. If one part suffers, every part suffers with it*" (1 Corinthians 12:25–26). This book will strengthen your resolve to do something about it.

October 2008
Gerrards Cross

Stephen Gaukroger is an international speaker and author, Chairman of Open Doors UK Council of Reference.

Prologue

by Mike Burnard

The servant listened attentively to the disturbing news from abroad. The city was in ruins and the people he loved were abandoned, afflicted and broken. As the man of God listened his heart was filled with compassion and he had one concern and one concern only: "How are my brothers and sisters, those of the faith? How are those that escaped, which are left of the captivity there and are in great affliction?" (Nehemiah 1). Indeed, this was Nehemiah, a man whose heart was with his people, the people of God. He wept as he listened and knew that he, a simple servant in the king's palace, had a mandate and a God-given responsibility to become the answer to the prayers of the afflicted. He was the man to bring along change. He needed to respond and he needed to do so immediately.

Nehemiah is a testimony of an ordinary man with an extraordinary God. He is a telling example of a man who heard of a need and then reacted in obedience – a person just like you and me.

The book that you are about to read will provide information similar to the news that Nehemiah received. We need to apply the same empathy, principles and practical applications that flowed from this servant of God. The first thing

Nehemiah did was to ask questions: *"How are my brothers and sisters, those of the faith?"* We need to be informed about worldwide events and how they affect people. How else will we be able to apply God's commands if we do not know what is happening in the world today? We need to ask questions about current events and understand the pain within the Body of Christ. This is not an option. When one member suffers the whole body suffers with it (1 Corinthians 12:26). But knowledge alone is not enough. Reading this book might equip you as a reader to a better understanding of Christians who share the cross of Christ, but it will still not make a difference in their lives. Knowledge brings responsibility. Nehemiah didn't just ask questions and then sit back to wait for answers. The first reaction of Nehemiah was to weep. A heart for mission is born in tears. Jesus never spoke about the lost, the needy and the weak without being filled with compassion. The thousands that are persecuted today for *our* faith have names. They need and deserve our empathy.

But, once again, Nehemiah went one step further. He prayed and put feet to his faith. He did not consider his position, his comfort or his safety. He counted the cost, knew the dangers and trusted God. Our comfort and freedom demands from us to be informed, aware and awake! May this book inspire you to action. May your heart be filled with compassion and inspiration to servanthood, especially to those of the household of faith.

> *"Therefore, as we have opportunity, let us do good to all people, especially to those who belong to the family of believers."*
> (Galatians 6:10)

Mike Burnard is Vice President, Development, Open Doors International and has been with Open Doors for twenty-one years.

Introduction

Of all the assignments that I have worked on in the past, this is by far *the* project that I have felt most privileged to have been given. It is also the one that has caused me the most pain and trauma as I have sat and listened to the ordeals that fellow Christians have endured, sometimes by their families, sometimes by the State, and, saddest of all, sometimes by fellow Christians. Months after my first interviews with the people mentioned in this book I was still deeply disturbed by the things that they shared with me, which some did at great emotional cost.

On several occasions I have been the first person who they have felt able to tell their story to. Often their experiences would be told in a rush of words, followed by tears as they mentally relived their ordeal. It wasn't unusual for me to pray before and after the interviews I was conducting, and often several times in between, as they fought to find composure before continuing their story.

Christians in the West who have grown up with the stories of persecution of believers behind the Iron or Bamboo curtains have probably secretly heaved a sigh of relief that it was not something that they personally had to face. They know that on a global scale it is the *exception* if Christians are not persecuted, not the norm. Each year Open Doors produces its World Watch List and handbook of prayer containing details of the top fifty countries where the persecution of Christians is most

acute. Entitled *Persecuted but Not Forsaken* it shows that North
Korea, Saudi Arabia, Iran and Maldives head the list, and
includes many Muslim and communist countries. You can
obtain further details online at www.opendoorsuk.org.

Although persecution appeared to be something that only
happened to other Christians in other parts of the world, it
now seems that persecution is beginning to knock on the door
of the Western Church. And just as every country has
characteristics peculiar to the area in which it lies, so the
persecution of the Western Church looks and is different from
that which other parts of the Church has experienced in the
past. Persecution of Western Christians is more subtle, more
secretive and often happens behind closed doors. But it is real
enough and is starting to affect more and more believers as
they seek to live godly lives.

So is this just a spiritual blip, something that has appeared and
will disappear just as quickly? Or is it the first signs of something
that will eventually affect all those Christians in the West who
want to stay true to their Christian beliefs? Should we ignore
what appears at first glance to be a small earth tremor, or start
to make preparations for the earthquake that could shake the
Western Church out of its age old complacency?

Whatever the right answer to that question is, the *fact* is
that persecution is real enough for the people mentioned in
this book and for the many others whose stories will have to
wait for another time. As you read the following chapters,
don't expect a lot of happy endings. They are not those kind of
stories. It's not that kind of book. Having said that, I truly
believe that the horrors that some believers have had to
endure will eventually be *eternally* rewarded when they meet
Jesus their Saviour face to face who has, I am sure, indescrib-
able blessings in store for them.

One thing that I was very aware of as I spoke to those
who had been through incredible difficulties is how so often
faith increases rather than decreases through persecution, in

whatever form that takes. And how Jesus knows exactly how to direct, instruct or comfort just at the right time, in the most wonderful way. And there are as many examples of that fact as there are stories to tell.

It goes without saying that key elements of the stories in this book, like locations and the names of people, have been altered to protect their identity. But the stories themselves have not been embellished in any way. It happened just the way it is told, revealing all the sadness, pain and distress that these modern day saints went through, whilst other parts of the Church were completely ignorant of what was going on. As the book of Ecclesiastes remind us, there is *"a time to be silent"*, but it goes on to say *"and a time to speak"* (Ecclesiastes 3:7). I believe that the time to give these persecuted believers an opportunity to speak is now.

Come with me as I introduce you to some remarkable people with some amazing stories to tell. "Could persecution come to the West?" we sometimes ask. The stark answer is that for some it has arrived already, and is not likely to go away anytime soon.

PART 1

When the Fire Fell

A "Big Top" tent in a holiday town was the entrance to the Kingdom of God for Fred, but it was the uninformed and thoughtless actions of fellow Christians that drove him away from God for years. But God loved Fred Hammond enough to speak to him directly – even though Fred had turned his back on God twenty-one years before – bringing him back into the church with a new zeal and vitality. What was to eventually follow involved threats and intimidation that would allow Fred and his church to discover God's love for them and those that hated them in a much deeper way. This is his story.

A week by the coast! What could be better than that I thought to myself as I walked along the seashore with my mates. We were all in our mid teens, grateful to get away from the city fumes of Leeds and enjoy all that the Devon coast had to offer. We were all from working-class families and time away from the normal cut and thrust of life was a real treat.

It was on about day three that we saw a big marquee being erected near the shore. One of the gang said it was probably a circus coming to town, but I knew that the tent was not big enough for anything like that. Then, when we saw the notices going up we realised that it was something to do with

Christianity. We passed it again the next evening as we took a
stroll along the beach, trying to decide what to do to entertain
ourselves that night. As we approached the tent some chap
started to try and persuade us to go in. We had no intention of
doing anything like that, and told him so – but then on the
spur of the moment we agreed to anyway, just to send
the whole thing up. But God had the last laugh, because that
night I heard and understood the Gospel message for the first
time. By the end of the evening I had asked God to forgive my
sins and Jesus to take control of my life.

My family didn't know what to make of me when I arrived
home. At best they thought I would probably return from
holiday with a suntan on my face and sand in my shoes.
Instead, I told them that I had become a Christian! My
encounter with God had an immediate impact upon my life.
I was attending the local Grammar School but suddenly
Religious Education lessons became a problem. My teacher
tried to explain away every miracle in the Bible, whereas I had
no problem in believing that if, for instance, God wanted to
give manna to the Israelites six days a week for forty years as
they travelled in the wilderness, He could do so. And if the sea
that Moses led the children of Israel through was so shallow as
to not need a miracle, as my teacher had suggested, it logically
meant that Pharaoh's mighty army had somehow drowned in
very shallow water! In the end, to pass my exams, I made a
deal with the headmaster. I would answer the questions in the
way my teacher expected them to be answered – and then
give the version that I believed to be true!

Mum and Dad saw the change in my life and just six
months after I became a Christian they gave their hearts to
Jesus too. We all started to attend a local church which
advocated a very strict lifestyle and was very hot on reading
and memorising whole chunks of the Bible. There was
nothing wrong with either of those things of course, except
that this particular church was so restrictive that on one

occasion I was publicly criticised and condemned in a Sunday morning service for going to see a film which I needed to view in order to complete a project at school. The film in question had a U certificate and was not questionable in any way, although it did have a vaguely religious theme. My public humiliation before the whole assembly shook my confidence in church and I started to be disillusioned by the way that some Christians acted, influenced as I now believe they were by a wrong understanding of the Bible. My love for God started to fall away and before I knew it, I was back in the secular world again – with a vengeance.

I started to play hard and drink hard. My lifestyle now was far from Christian. I wanted to put as much space between myself and the church as I could. I married, had children, ran several pubs over the years, and never gave God a thought.

Then twenty-one years after I had been humiliated in church by well-intentioned Christian people, I was on holiday again, this time with my wife in a caravan in Norfolk. It was late one night and she had fallen asleep. I was trying to do the same, when suddenly the Holy Spirit started to speak to me! I heard His voice and over several hours He began to show me where a character flaw had developed at a key stage in my youth, something I was completely unaware of. He then showed me that I needed to forgive those who were involved, just as He had forgiven me. He then took me through the incident that had happened at church twenty-one years before, pointing out where others had erred, but showing me also how I could have handled it better. After all that was over, He said that although I had turned my back on Him for twenty-one years, He had never left me or forsaken me, and had been there with me through it all. I felt dreadful when I realised the pain I had caused to God by my rejection of Him, then so grateful that He cared enough to bring me back into fellowship with Him.

After that amazing experience the Lord would wake me very early each morning, and although I had long since discarded my Bible, He would bring a scripture to my remembrance and talk to me about it. I was getting my own personal tuition from the Holy Spirit! My wife, who was far from the Christian faith at the time, would wake up and see me with a huge smile on my face and say, "He's been talking to you again hasn't He?" Within six months, she too had given her life to God.

We both got back into the Christian community and using my pub landlord experience we opened a non-alcoholic pub, an innovation at the time, and one which God used in an amazing way to bring people to salvation. Within a few years I was the Pastor of a small but lively church in a poor and deprived area of Liverpool. Most of the congregation of around fifty people were either past retirement age or on some kind of government benefit. Only about three people were in full-time employment, one of them being my wife.

Our church building was in an area which was fairly heavily populated with Muslim immigrants. That didn't bother us and it didn't seem to bother them. In fact, there were certain occasions when they would stop us in the street and ask for prayer. Sometimes they even came to the church to be prayed for and I recall several times when God graciously healed them of terminal illnesses.

But then we discovered that a Muslim group had acquired land at the back of our church. Again, this was not a problem as far as we were concerned, but it did become a problem when they then approached us to buy our church building. As it happened, the Lord had told me some time before this happened that He wanted us to move to a bigger building, but when this approach was made I knew the timing was not right, so I had to decline their offer to purchase the premises at that time. That obviously didn't go down too well because the next thing we knew cars belonging to our church members started to be vandalised, with leaflets attached to windscreens stating, *Allah is the one true God – leave now.* Car doors were kicked in and windscreens smashed. The challenge as I saw it was how we responded to what was happening. I called a church meeting and reminded our folks that they must respond in love, however frustrating things might be, because how we reacted to this would be how our attackers saw Christ.

"Get insurance damage from your insurance company if you want," I told them, "but one day your car is only going to be a lump of rusting metal anyway. The people who are doing these things are eternal beings who need to see the love of God in our lives and theirs." The church responded well to my message.

The following month a new tactic was tried. The doors of the church building were daubed with the word "ALLAH" and once again the same leaflets were found. We chose to ignore it all and continued to pray for those responsible. Then a couple of weeks later, the whole thing was ratcheted up a few more notches to a new and dangerous level during our weekly Bible study, which we held in the church.

The church building was basically just one big room. It had a front door leading into a very small hall, with another door with a glass panel above it which opened into the big meeting room. That Tuesday evening, as I was teaching from the Bible, I suddenly heard the glass panel above the door breaking. That was followed by a loud whooshing sound. Because I had watched so many action drama films in the years before I came back to the Lord I knew immediately what had happened. We had been fire bombed. Through the hole where the glass at the top of the doors had been I could easily see the petrol-fed flames dancing around in the entrance hall! It had all happened very quickly, with no prior warning.

Without explaining why, I told the congregation, who were all sitting facing away from the door, to quickly pick up their belongings and make their way out of the building via the emergency exit. I got a few puzzled looks, but people did what I asked of them, quickly and quietly. We were all able to leave

without any harm or danger to ourselves. When we got out
onto the street, I explained what had happened and then I ran
round to the front of the building. The doors were on fire,
licking around the word "ALLAH" that had been daubed
there the night before. I informed the Police, as was my duty,
but they seemed more embarrassed than anything else. They
knocked on a few doors up and down the street, but basically
that was all the action that was taken. Once some of the
elderly members of the congregation realised what had
happened it really shook them up. They couldn't quite believe
what they were living through. But the saga was not yet over.

A couple of months later a caravan that we used for
evangelistic outreaches was overturned, causing damage
inside and out. It seemed that anything that we owned that
was used for the Lord's work was fair game to those who
were against us. A few days after that, when I left my house
one morning and began to walk down the garden path
towards my car, which was parked in the road, I noticed that
it looked quite dirty. Making a mental note to take it to the
local car wash as soon as I could, it was only as I got round
the other side of the vehicle that I realised that the "dirt" was
actually smoke, and that my car had been fire bombed and the
back window smashed in. It had happened in the night, but
because our house had double-glazed windows we had not
heard a thing. Again, a computer generated leaflet had been
left stating *Allah is the One True God – you must leave – it could be
you next.*

The next move of those who wanted us out of the area was
to position themselves near the church, then as the church
members were approaching the building they would be spat
on by Muslim youth and even young children who called
them "dirty Christians". At the time all this was happening
my father was living with us and was sleeping downstairs
because of his chronic health condition. He could hardly walk
and began to get concerned as to what could happen if

they decided to firebomb the house, which thankfully never happened.

I was interested to see the effect of all these things on the church members. It actually became a time when we grew as a fellowship, learning to trust God and to show our love for Him, and others outside the church, much more. No one wants or looks for persecution, but when it comes, God very often uses it in a powerful way.

It was, of course, complete intimidation and designed to demoralise us, to put so much fear into us that we would leave. But we would not be intimidated. However, we did ultimately sell the building to the Muslim group that wanted it, not because of what they had done, but because the Lord had said before it all stated to happen that we were to move, but in His time.

The way God worked was quite amazing. Not only did He show me exactly the amount I was to ask for the church building that this Islamic group wanted, but He showed me the building we were to move into before it came up for sale. The sum I told the Muslims they had to pay was much higher than what they first offered. I told them honestly that God had given me a figure, but it was one that they needed to discover for themselves, and when they discovered what it was we could talk. They had never been presented with a situation like that before, but I think they sensed that I was being totally truthful with them and responded accordingly. When they eventually came up with the figure that God had revealed to me, I was very frank with them and told them all the faults that the building survey had revealed, but they said they didn't care – they just wanted the building because of its location, it was pointing in the right direction, i.e. towards Mecca. As soon as the figure was finally agreed they wanted us out of the building immediately, but I told them that we would only go when we had another permanent building to go into.

The following Monday, as I was driving past the building that the Lord had shown me one day would be ours, I saw a "For Sale" sign going up outside! Getting in touch with the estate agents, I then offered a sum of money to buy the building, only to be told that my offer was way too low. Again, it was a figure that God had given me, so I knew that eventually it would be the figure we would pay. And after many twists and turns the figure was accepted, against all odds, and we moved into a much more suitable building for our growing needs.

I know that there are many decent, peace loving Muslims in this country today who just want to get on with their lives and let others get on with theirs. But there is also a hardcore of extremists, sometimes whipped up by persuasive clerics who incite impressionable youth to violent acts. The Christian's strongest defence is love. We must show the love of God to these people as often and in as many ways as we can. Christians are on their firmest ground when they do two things: obey God's Word and show love to all, including their enemies.

Some of the problems that we faced went away when the old building was sold. That said, our new building had all its windows smashed soon after we moved in, and our members still sometimes get spat upon and called dirty Christians when they come to the church. But through it all we have become strong in God. We have seen people healed and brought to faith locally and great things have happened when we have sent teams out to foreign lands. In the end, all persecution does is bring us closer to the one true God, who loves us all with an everlasting love.

Storm in a Coffee Cup

All Margaret wanted to do was to help a fellow Christian who was going through a difficult time trying to bring up young children on her own and struggling with bouts of depression. But a friendly chat over a cup of coffee after work led to Margaret being suspended from her work for eight weeks, when the powers that be discovered that Margaret was a Christian and had encouraged members of her church to help her friend who was plainly not coping. Then, a real threat that she would lose her job and livelihood loomed on the horizon ... This is her story.

I've always loved my job as a Health Visitor. It's a great way of meeting people and helping them in a very practical way. I've been a Christian since I was ten, growing up in the kind of environment that caused people to want to help their friends and neighbours if they could. Mine was a happy childhood, in spite of the fact that my dad left home when I was very young. However, my mother was a committed Christian who taught me in the ways of God. In a very simple but real way I gave my heart to the Lord at a fairly early age and have never regretted the decision that I made.

After leaving school I got a job in the National Health Service, initially as a State Registered Nurse and then as a midwife before becoming a Health Visitor. I developed a special interest in mental health issues, having suffered from depression for a while after experiencing a couple of very traumatic events. So, when the vicar of the Anglican church that I had joined asked me to keep a friendly eye on Sally, a lady who had recently moved to the area with her three young children after her husband walked out on her, and who was finding life a little difficult, it was something that I was happy to do.

Sally and I became good friends and because I had never married or had children of my own, her children were special to me too. What started out as a commission from the vicar turned into a genuine friendship, even to the point of Sally asking me to become godmother and legal guardian to her children should anything ever happen to her, a request to which I readily agreed and which cemented our friendship even more.

When I consented to be legal guardian to Sally's children it seemed more of an honour than a role I would ever have to act out. But as time went on I began to wonder more and more if it might become an actual possibility. Sally found the burden of looking after her children, one of whom had learning difficulties, and the rejection of her husband too much to bear, and she started to go into a spiral of depression, causing her to sink into an emotional quicksand which she had no idea how to escape from.

By this time I was leading a church support group for people suffering with, or recovering from, depression. They became aware of Sally's problem and started to help when-ever they could. But it was to me that Sally turned more often than not, sometimes telephoning me as frequently as fourteen times throughout the day and night. I knew, as a health visitor myself, that the friendship that she was receiving from me and others at church was not enough – she needed professional help. In spite of that I didn't act out a role of health visitor to

Sally, making sure that all that I did was strictly in line with just being a friend to her.

But I grew more and more concerned as I watched Sally finding it increasingly difficult to cope. The day arrived when I decided that I needed to do something positive to get her some professional help, so I took the bull by the horns and phoned Sally's health visitor.

After explaining that I was a health visitor myself, I said that I was a good friend of Sally's and that I was concerned about her irrational behaviour which was becoming more frequent. The health visitor seemed concerned at what I told her and she suggested that we meet to discuss the situation further, a suggestion that in the end never actually materialised. Although I felt encouraged after this conversation nothing seemed to be put in place to help her and Sally's behaviour became more disturbing. A little while after that conversation Sally was found on the street in the middle of the night, in the pouring rain with her very young child. Someone had the presence of mind to phone the vicar and he made sure that she and the baby were taken care of. Had he not taken some positive action on that occasion I am not sure what would have happened to her. The group at church that were trying to help her also discovered around that time that sometimes her children were not being fed properly and her condition began to be a worry to us all.

After talking the situation through with Sally and the vicar, I again rang her health visitor and expressed my concerns. At the beginning of my conversation with her she seemed alarmed and sympathetic as she listened to what I had to say. Then, to put her fully in the picture, I told her of the amount of support the family was getting from the church. It was at that point that the attitude of Sally's health visitor changed. Her tone suddenly became very hostile and she told me to tell the church to "back off" and to leave things to the health professionals!

Even if that had been practical, which it wasn't as Sally was still telephoning many times a day because she just couldn't cope without our support, she was also a friend who was turning to me and the rest of the church group for help. I knew that I had always made a point of not discussing her children in a professional way with Sally, but being simply a friend to her and a caring godmother to the children.

Time moved on and it was suggested by her health visitor that Sally should attend parenting classes. That was a wise suggestion, but Sally was very fearful about going. It is not an unusual reaction for someone in her condition and in my capacity as health visitor when trying to get my clients to attend this type of class I would actually take them to their sessions, to give them the extra boost that they needed. I knew which evening Sally was due to attend and I wondered if she would find the courage when the time came for her to go on her own. The next morning she was on the phone to me and I naturally asked if she had managed to attend the parenting classes the night before, and she said she had. I congratulated her on her efforts – I knew it had taken a lot of courage on her part to turn up. She then asked if I would go round to her house that evening so that she could tell me more.

"Sorry Sally, I've got house group tonight – but I tell you what, I'll pop in for a cup of coffee before I go if you like," I added, as I sensed that she was disappointed that she would not be able to see me at all. I did pop round that evening, had a quick cup of coffee, listened to what she had to say, and then made my way to the house group, never suspecting for a moment the problems that would arise from this simple and brief visit to my friend.

The following day Sally was talking to her health visitor and in the course of the conversation mentioned the fact that I had called round for a coffee the evening before. Her health visitor became very angry, wrongly assuming that I was trying to take over her professional role. She reported me to my line manager and without further ado I was suspended from work and accused of gross misconduct, breach of professional boundaries and breach of confidentiality! I was devastated, but there was nothing I could do once the official wheels had been set in motion. Sally's health visitor seemed to find it impossible to separate the fact that although I was a health visitor, I was also Sally's friend and was visiting her as a friend and fellow Christian to encourage her.

The action that was now being brought against me started to have an impact upon the church. They too were criticised for what they had been doing to help Sally. They were labelled as "do gooders" and "interfering" because my vicar had phoned the social services and not the health visitor when Sally became extremely disturbed. Following that call she was admitted to a psychiatric unit for four weeks while the children went into care for a period of about six months. I have to say that without the church involvement things could have been very bad indeed for Sally.

Most of those at church who had tried to help Sally were confused as to why they should be criticised and I should be suspended. There was very little I could say to clarify the situation and I suppose it's possible that some people thought I must have done more than I had said for such severe action to be taken against me.

Meanwhile, I was told by my manager that I had to separate church from work and that I shouldn't have friends living in the same authority that I worked in! I was also told that I was not to have any contact with Sally or her children, something which has caused me great pain. She was after all a long-standing friend of mine and I am legal guardian and godmother to the children. All that no longer seemed to count for anything any more as far as the authorities were concerned.

After eight long and tense weeks of being suspended from work I was called to attend a formal disciplinary hearing. Much to my relief the case against me was thrown out, but there was a point leading up to the hearing when I was informed that I might be reported to the Nursing Council, which, had that have happened meant that I could not only have lost my job but also my nursing registration, which would have prevented me from working for the National Health Service again.

Although my case was thrown out by the disciplinary hearing, my manager continued to bully me, stating that she would act in the same way again if the same kind of situation arose. I didn't make a formal complaint against her, but I did start to make notes of the conversations that we had together and I told her that if there was just one more incident of bullying on my manager's part I would make a formal complaint against her. Shortly after that she resigned from her job.

If you think that what happened to me is some kind of bizarre, isolated case I can assure you that it isn't. A friend of mine was a health visitor in a totally different part of the country, but was also bullied due to her beliefs. She was asked to do things that she felt were wrong and so refused. She too was subjected to a disciplinary hearing but decided that she could not cope with the stress of it all and resigned. Her "crime" was that while shopping in the city centre she met by chance a client of hers, a young mother with problems. As they were talking, the mother burst into tears and so my friend bought her a cup of coffee and sat with her until she was calm enough to be left. The mother was very grateful for the kindness that she had been shown and told another health professional what my friend had done. Unfortunately this person did not agree that this had been a good thing to do and reported what had happened to my friend's manager, which resulted in the disciplinary hearing.

But to get back to my own circumstances, I know that my church fellowship has found it hard to help people in the way they were doing before all this happened. A certain amount of trust has been lost. Unsurprisingly, Sally no longer attends church on a regular basis, and sadly some people in the church now find it difficult when she does. I am sure that had we not been a church group and had I not been a Christian involved in a caring ministry the criticism that we were subjected to would not have happened. Sally was not and never had been a client of mine, nor did I ever treat her in that way. The only good thing to come out of all of this as far as I can see is the way my church family supported me throughout it all. They turned up at my hearing and prayed for me, they wrote letters of support and showed me great kindness. But the whole thing has left its scar on me and my church family.

In spite of all that the Bible teaches on helping those in need, which I believe is every Christian's duty, the whole situation has made me more wary in the way I approach situations and the advice I give to others. I tend to tell other people doing the kind of work that I am still doing to take notes and be on their guard if they feel they are going into uncertain areas of their work.

Maybe one day I and my church will once again have that wholehearted attitude to those around us in society who are in so much need. But to be honest, I don't think it's going to happen any time soon.

A Postcard from Heaven

Language was the first of many problems Lela was confronted with when she first came to England. Soon after leaving school she was forced into an arranged marriage and when children started to come along she was increasingly confined to the home. After a supernatural encounter with Jesus just before her third child was born Lela wanted to know more about this person who the Muslim faith said was just a prophet. But the price for knowing more about Jesus became too high – until she saw a postcard which set her on a journey of heartache and tears resulting in a powerful relationship with the Man of Sorrows and the Prince of Peace.

My early life was spent in Indonesia and it was a good life. My mother's parents owned land and she inherited some of it when she got married. My grandparents lived in a lovely big house with a wonderful garden and lots of servants to do all the work.

However, work was not plentiful for everyone and my father heard that if one was prepared to travel abroad there were many opportunities to become rich. Soon he was on his way to Britain and it wasn't long before I started to miss him and wonder when he was coming home. My sister laughed at my innocent question and told me that Dad wouldn't be returning, but that one day we would be going to where he had travelled to. I could not believe what she was telling me, but sure enough the time came when Mum packed up our belongings and we all headed for the airport and a new life in England. I was just eight years old and could never have guessed how this move would ultimately completely change the course of my life.

Dad had found work in the North East of England. I couldn't get used to the grey leaden skies day after day, which often produced much rain. I longed for the blue skies of Indonesia and the brilliant sun that used to wake me up each morning. The house that we moved into was small and terraced, with a tiny back yard and an outside toilet. That was the only kind of accommodation that we could afford.

All this was hard enough, but things became even more difficult when my sister and I started school. We soon discovered that we were the only Indonesian girls there and nobody spoke our language! When Mum realised that she arranged for a lady to come round to the house to teach us English and soon we were making ourselves known and understood to the rest of the class.

Islam was the faith I had been born into and was what we all practised as a family. When we moved to England that part of our life remained the same in spite of that fact that there was not a mosque near to where we were living. I first heard the name of Jesus uttered when the hymn *Onward, Christian Soldiers* was sung in our morning assembly. But it had little or no impact upon me and by the time I had reached secondary school, school assemblies no longer took place, so I did not hear anything more about Him from a Christian prospective. As a Muslim I had been taught that Jesus was just another prophet.

A few short months after leaving secondary school I was married off to a man who was much older than me chosen for me by my parents. I had no say in the matter. It was not long before our first child was on its way, quickly followed by the second which inevitably caused me to be more and more confined to the house.

It was just before I was due to give birth to my third child that I had my first encounter with Jesus. I was in the delivery suite of my local hospital, waiting for the baby to be born, and my contractions were coming with increasing frequency and pain. I tried to be brave, but I began to wonder how much more pain I could endure. Suddenly I realised that I was looking at myself lying on the table, watching what was going on from a vantage point somewhere near the ceiling! I knew that this was not possible, yet it was happening. Then suddenly I was aware of the outline of a man, who was emitting an incredibly bright light, standing in the corner of the room. The light was so bright that it was impossible to see His face. Somehow I knew this to be Jesus, although He did not speak to me or me to Him. I had been worried about the birth, but now I felt wonderfully calm. After my baby was born I haemorrhaged very badly, but even that did not make me afraid. I knew everything would be all right. But I could not understand why Jesus had appeared to me, a Muslim woman. I decided not to tell anyone what had happened, as I felt that no one that I knew would approve or understand what I had experienced.

Soon after I brought our third baby home my husband found better paid work in a different part of the country. I naturally presumed that we would be moving to where his new work was, but instead he told me that he had found a flat where he would live during the week and come back to me and the children at weekends. This sounded good in theory, but what actually happened was that he not only found a new job, but also began living with a woman from the town he was now working in. He was quite open about it all and I was just expected to accept this new arrangement, but of course it caused me great distress. This new situation meant that I was now bringing the children up virtually single handed. I went to see my family to see if they could offer me any advice and support. They were very unsympathetic. In fact, they piled all the blame on me, saying that my husband probably wouldn't have gone off with another woman if I had been a better wife! At first my husband came home every weekend, then this began to tail off until it got to the point where he rarely came back to see me and the children at all.

I began to get friendly with an English woman who lived nearby, someone I knew had always lived in the area, who I presumed, because she was white and English was a Christian. One day, plucking up all my courage, I mentioned to her the vision of Jesus that I had seen just before giving birth to my third child. This was the first time I had told this story to anyone. I just wanted to know what someone else made of it all. I realise now that she had very little spiritual knowledge because she said that as far as she was concerned, the fact that I had seen a vision of Jesus made me a Christian! My first reaction was to look at her in horror. Could what she was saying be true? I had no way of knowing. My next reaction was to feel offended. How could she say that? I was a good Muslim! I asked her not to tell anyone what I had told her, and not to say that I was a Christian again.

This conversation, however, did begin a sort of spiritual journey for me, in spite of the fact that my friend was so ill informed. I began to become more and more curious about Jesus and I secretly wanted to know more about Him. How that was going to work out I did not know. I decided to give the problem to God in prayer and see what He might work out. It was about that time that I started attending a part-time course on community matters at the local college. One of the women who I began to relate to was a Christian, but had been a Hindu. She in turn introduced me to another woman who had been a Muslim before she became a Christian. Soon she was asking me if I would like to go along to her church and I readily agreed, thinking that this would be the way I would discover more about Jesus.

However, the church she went to, whilst they loved to sing very lively hymns and were totally into praising and worshipping God, on the teaching side they lacked any real depth or substance. They were all having a great time singing and clapping, but I couldn't relate to much that went on in the services. All I wanted was a quiet conversation with someone who would be able to answer all the questions I had about Jesus! However, I was determined not to be put off, and over the next few weeks I did learn more about Him, especially about the love and compassion He had for all those that He came into contact with. I was starting to love Him more and more, but at this point I was going along to church secretly. I knew I would be in even more serious trouble with my family if they discovered that I was attending a church.

A few weeks later I got an unexpected phone call from my mum, inviting me and the children over for lunch. I gladly accepted. As we sat on the bus watching the world go by, I hoped that this meal would start a new chapter in my relationship with Mum and through her, the rest of the family. But when we arrived, I could not smell any food cooking which I thought was a bit odd. Indonesian food smells wonderful when it is cooking and its aromas are hard to disguise. I soon discovered why I could smell no food. None had been prepared. Instead, Mum showed me into her living room where my aunt, who was a very strict Muslim woman, was waiting to speak to me. She said that they had discovered that I was attending a church and wanted to know what was going on. I said simply and honestly that I had started to go to a church because I wanted to know more about Jesus who I had discovered is the Son of God. When I said that they both got very angry, saying that Jesus was a prophet, but nothing more. They said that the people at the church had brainwashed me and that God could never have a son and as a Muslim I ought to know that, and remember the teachings of Muhammad. When I said that I still wanted to continue going to church in spite of their advice, they became enraged. They took hold of me, opened a door and roughly pushed me down some stone stairs into a cellar, saying that they would not let me out until I denounced my statements about Jesus and promised to stop attending church. I heard a bolt being drawn across the door as I landed heavily on the cold stone floor of the cellar. There was no way of getting out until they unbolted the door.

The cellar was dirty, dark and damp and full of horrible insects. A terrible musty smell made me want to be sick. As my eyes became accustomed to the light I wondered if I was also sharing this awful place with rats and mice. The thought made my flesh creep. But worse than my own physical discomfort was the fact that I could hear my little children crying for me. All I wanted to do was to get out of this miserable pit and go home with my children. But I knew I would not be released until I promised not to go to church any more. Several hours went by, when I could hear my children becoming more and more distressed. In the end I could stand it no more. I was putting my small children through a terrible ordeal and it wasn't fair on them. And as the afternoon turned into evening I could also hear my mum crying. She was obviously upset that my aunt had been so hard on me and wanted me to be released again. A feeling of desperation suddenly swept over me. I banged on the door, shouting to my mum and aunt that if they let me out I would promise not go to church any more or read my Bible or try to find out anything more about Jesus. I had been locked up for eight long hours. I was released from my prison within seconds. But it was liberty with a price tag attached. I knew that the promises I had made under duress would have to be kept. I had begun to love Jesus, but I loved my mum and my children even more and couldn't bear to make them upset.

It was with a very heavy heart that I then had to tell my Christian friends that I would no longer be coming along to church. Their reaction to my news saddened me. They told me that I was committing the biggest sin by turning my back on Jesus. In fairness to them, I don't believe they had any idea of the pressures that someone like me from the Muslim community comes under when they turn to Jesus as their Saviour. But even so I found their reaction difficult to handle. Instead of coming to see me and offering me support in the struggles that I was now facing, they just stopped having any contact with me, leaving me completely alone and isolated.

But although fellow Christians might have given up on me, God certainly hadn't. And He chose a most unusual way of showing that He still loved me. As I was visiting a single parent group some twelve months later, I happened to see a postcard with a picture of Jesus on it. I felt startled as I looked at Jesus, looking at me, and as I continued to stare at it, I heard a still small voice deep inside me saying, "Come back to Me – I miss you."

That was all I needed. The very next Sunday found me back in church, but this time things were different. I felt stronger as a person somehow; more ready to take what might be thrown at me. I asked Jesus to come and live in my heart and be with me forever. Now I knew that I would need all the spiritual help that I could get and so the next step in my spiritual journey was to get baptised, which I did very soon after.

The day after I got baptised I went to see my mum to tell her what I had done. I had after all made a promise to her which I had broken and I wanted her to know why I had done that. I don't think at first my mum could believe what I was saying when I told her that I had not only become a Christian but I had also been baptised. But when it did sink in, which didn't take long, she got extremely angry, slapping me around the face and crying hysterically. Then my sister arrived and she joined in, throwing a lot of abuse my way. There was no way of talking to them rationally, so I left as quickly as I could, planning to return a few days later, when I hoped to approach the subject again in a calmer atmosphere.

Only a few days had gone by, but my mum looked pale and drawn and had lost quite a bit of weight. She told me that she had gone to the mosque and told them that her daughter had gone crazy, without saying in what way, and they had given her some water for me to drink. My mum said that if I drank the water I would become a good Muslim again.

I sensed that this was some kind of test and that I need not be afraid of water from a mosque. I took it from my mum and drank every last drop, telling my mum that Jesus is stronger than any water that she might be able to give me. When Mum saw that indeed the water was having no influence on me, she again became abusive and I again had to leave the house.

Soon all my family knew that I had become a Christian and been baptised, and I was called to a big family conference. Several of my aunties were there, as well as my mum who had just been discharged from hospital because she had been suffering from stress. Everyone was glaring at me, apart from my mum, who would not even look at me, which I found very upsetting.

Soon my aunts were going through all the reasons why I should return to Islam and all the reasons why Christianity was totally the wrong faith to follow. When I started to defend my actions, they changed their strategy.

"How much money do you want from us, so that you will deny your faith?" they asked. I told them that no amount of money would make me do that. They looked surprised at my reply and then went into a huddle before coming up with a new proposition.

"OK, but if we offered to buy you a house, would you deny your faith?" they asked. I assured them that I would not. They began to get exasperated. They then said that they would find me a new husband and when I still shook my head they said that maybe lots of gold jewellery would do the trick. I knew that these were not just idle promises and they could produce all the things that they were offering if necessary. But I turned down every inducement in favour of Jesus. Then they played their trump card.

"Lela, here is your mum. You have to choose. You can have a relationship with your mum or one with Jesus. But you can't have both. You decide."

This was terrible. I never thought it would get to this. I looked at my mum who still had not acknowledged me and was now silently weeping. The pressure on us both was enormous. I was a young Christian who had not received too much help or support from my fellow believers. Now I was being asked to give up my relationship with my mum, who I loved so much. But there was only one way I could go.

"I love my mum," I heard myself saying, "but I love Jesus and can't deny Him whatever you say to me."

At that point, the mood in the meeting changed again and I saw real anger in the eyes of those who had been talking to me. "All right, we have tried to be reasonable with you, but obviously you have been brainwashed. So we warn you that if you don't return to the Muslim faith you will have to leave town and we will take your children from you and send them to Indonesia." Soon after that the meeting ended with nothing resolved on either side.

I made my way home in a turmoil. This was not the only big issue that I was dealing with. During the time that all this was going on, my daughter, who was now in her mid teens, had run away from home, and when my husband, who I was still technically married to, heard about this he said that because she had done that she had brought disgrace upon the family and if he found out where she was hiding he would kill her. And I knew he meant it.

Fortunately, I found her before he did, but the Police said that they could not protect her if she remained living with me in that area, so our only option was to move to a new place where we could not be found. A friend knew of a house that was empty in a different location and even knew of someone with a van who would be able to transport all my belongings there for me. In spite of all that, I went to bed that night with a very heavy heart. As I tossed and turned I kept thinking that I now had a husband who no longer loved me, a mother who had disowned me and a daughter who might be murdered by her own father. And now I had to leave all that was familiar and move to a different area where I knew no one.

But as I slept that night I had a dream and in that dream Jesus came to me. I started to ask Him why all this was happening to me and where all the peace and joy was that the Christian life promises. He didn't answer any of my questions. He just looked at me, called me by my name, and said, "My peace I leave with you." And that is exactly what happened. I suddenly felt this incredible peace come over me and when I woke up it was still with me. I knew that it was right to move and that everything was going to be okay. However, when I started to pray about the van that had been promised to transport all my worldly goods, the Lord told me I would not need it, as He wanted me to leave everything behind. Everything!

"But Lord," I pleaded, "I'm a single parent. I could never afford to replace my furniture, my fridge-freezer, my pots and pans, all the things I own." But He did not respond to my pleadings. He had spoken and I knew I had to be obedient. So all I needed to do was to pack clothes for myself and my children. The Lord had said He would provide everything else that we needed.

The day came for me to leave. There was just one last thing I had to do before I left. I asked my friend to drive me round to my mum's house. I needed to say goodbye to her. She was not there when I arrived and my dad and sister would not let me into the house. I sat in the car with my friend and waited for her to return. After a little while I saw her coming down the road, weighed down with groceries she had bought from the shops. I jumped out of the car, and told her that I was leaving the area. She pleaded with me not to go, but to stay and return to the Muslim faith. She said that she had been told by another Muslim that because of what I had done she would not be able to go to heaven when she died. I told her I couldn't do what she asked but that I still loved her and it was then that she started to cry. So did I. At that point my sister came out of the house and began to be very abusive towards me. I told my mum to go inside, but she just stood there on the pavement crying. I didn't want to leave her like this. I pleaded with her to go inside, but again she refused. We had to drive off and leave her there, standing on the side of the road weeping. It was a terrible moment.

A few hours later we arrived at our new home. It was pleasant enough, but the rooms were completely bare. We had nothing other than our clothes. But I knew that Jesus had said that was how it was to be. I felt relaxed and at peace about the whole situation, even though I had no idea how it would be resolved. Events proved that I had no reason to be worried. Over the next few days all sorts of things started to arrive. I would leave the house to go shopping and return to see some household items had been left for me – cooking utensils, pots and pans, an iron and ironing board. Then a TV was delivered – along with an envelope with money inside. Then some furniture and a fridge-freezer – and I couldn't help noticing that it was much better than the one I had left behind. Everything I needed was provided over a very short period, right down to needle and thread. My youngest son was totally impressed.

"Wow, Mum, it's all come in, just like you said it would, just because you prayed." I nodded at him, with a big smile on my face, happy that he was acknowledging God's part in all of this, but not ready for his next comment. "So, are you going to be praying that we win the lottery next, Mum?"

God had spoken to the Christian community in the area to provide the things that I needed and they were wonderful. But understanding and accepting me as a person was far more difficult for them to handle. Noreen was my one and only contact in the area and she started taking me to the church that she went to, which was fairly traditional and formal, something that I was not used to. For the first few weeks nobody called me by name, but just referred to me as "Noreen's friend". Fellowship was limited to a few brief minutes after a Sunday morning service and then I had no contact with anyone until the following Sunday. I felt so alone. I longed for my house to be used for house groups or prayer groups or whatever, but the offer was never taken up. God had given me a ministry of intercession which I wanted to use to help build up the church, but again I was sidelined. The truth was they didn't understand my background and maybe even felt threatened by my different colour skin, my accent, and the clothes I wore. But these things are all so superficial. I could never be a white, middle-class English lady, and to be honest I have no desire to be. All I know is that Jesus wants me to be true to myself. I just didn't know why my Christian brothers and sisters struggled with that so much.

Then ten years after arriving in the area I received some devastating news. I had been lacking in energy for a while and I made an appointment to see the doctor, expecting him to give me some kind of tonic. Instead I discovered that I had breast cancer. During those ten years my daughter had married, but I had not seen her children as she had not wanted me to. But when she heard the news she came to visit me, bringing the children with her which was a great joy. A few days later I had a phone call from my mum, the first time we had been in touch for ten years. I couldn't believe how she started the conversation.

"Lela, I hear you have cancer. Well, we won't be able to

come to your funeral you know if it's held in a Christian church!"

Those were her opening remarks to me. After ten years! I assured her that although I was not well I was still very much alive and had no intention of dying just yet! Amazingly though, she did come over to see me, and looked after me for a whole month while I had different tests and procedures in order to deal with the cancer. After I returned from the hospital on one occasion she told me that I would quickly discover that Jesus was no longer around. "I kicked Him out of the house," she told me with a smile on her face, "He no longer lives here now." She was shocked when I told her that Jesus didn't live in houses, but in the hearts of those who love Him. "He's living inside of me, Mum, and He always will be," I was able to say to her.

During the time she stayed with me I was able to show her the love of Jesus, even when she was praying to Allah five times a day! But at the end of that time she returned home with no real reconciliation between us.

Getting to know Jesus has been the most amazing thing that has happened to me. I sometimes hear Christians who have always lived in the West preach a message of joy and peace and prosperity and a stress free life if one becomes a Christian. Well, yes, Jesus does give peace and does provide all the things that we truly need. But for me and others I know like me, following Jesus has meant sacrifice, loneliness and many tears. Becoming a Christian has cost me my relationship with my natural family, my marriage and acceptance within my own natural community. My Christian friends still don't understand how all-embracing the Muslim faith is, and how shallow Christian fellowship can sometimes seem in comparison. Without His constant encouragement and help I am not sure that I could continue to survive spiritually. There are now other Christian women in the town where I live who were born in my part of the world that I sometimes relate to, but I don't want to live in a ghetto, only fellowshipping with those from my own background. Hopefully, the Lord will continue to break down the barriers that unintentionally divide Christians who originate from different parts of the globe, so that united together through the love of God we can all be dynamic parts in the Body of Jesus. The only way I have been able to come to terms with the things that others have done to me, intentionally or unintentionally, is to totally forgive them, whether they accept it or not. There is no other way. He has forgiven me totally for all my sins. I can do no less to those who have brought heartache and pain into my life. Love is always God's way, because He is love.

Festival to a Foreign God

When Trevor landed a job with a prominent UK Christian organisation, which involved helping people with drug problems, he was pleased and excited. But when someone joined the team who held different religious beliefs, Trevor and his Christian friends were told by their employers that they had to participate in a festival to a foreign god. He could never have guessed the difficulties he would then be plunged into when he tried to be true to his Christian beliefs...

Ever since I became a Christian I'd had a desire to help other people who were struggling in life. That motivation led me to work for ten years in a Christian run hostel for homeless alcoholics. I enjoyed the work, but felt after so many years that I needed a change, so I decided to lecture for a while. This didn't really work out, so I was pleased when I landed a job as a Mental Health Access Worker with a well known Christian organisation. I was told that my duties would involve helping those who were addicted to drink and drugs. I was looking forward to this new challenge and began to work the normal three month probationary period.

Everything started off well. I was working with four other Christians and we all related easily to each other. It was when a guy who happened to be a Hindu came to work with us that the problems began. He seemed a nice enough kind of chap, and as Christians we had no problem in working with him at all. But it was when the management decided that, because he was now part of the staff, Hindu festivals had to be observed within the organisation alongside Christian ones that the whole work atmosphere started to change. As Christians we all respected the right of people of other faiths to practise their religion, but we didn't personally want to get involved in their rituals and felt that we had biblical reasons for that stance.

At first, everything continued as usual, but then one day we were informed that the festival of Diwali was coming up and that all the staff, including the Christians, would be expected not only to prepare the food, but to participate in the celebrations as well! I made an appointment to see my boss to tell him that this flew in the face of what I felt was the right thing to do as a Christian. My boss maintained that he was not asking anyone to worship any other god other than their own, but could not, or would not see any other point of view. As Christians we all felt that because we were being asked to prepare the food and help others participate in the festivities we were, to all intents and purposes, being asked to take part ourselves. The management kept the pressure up and then, after a while, rather than make a fuss, two of my Christian colleagues decided to go along with what they had been told to do. But I still could not agree to what was being asked and I discovered the other Christian I was working with felt the same. We offered to stay on the premises and do other work instead, but stated that we could not get involved in a pagan religious festival as we strongly believed that this would be offensive in the eyes of God.

My "reward" for standing up for what I believed to be correct, based on the important biblical principle that Christians should not worship other gods, was swift and uncompromising. I was told that I was sacked from the organisation, that I was on a month's notice which I was not required to work, and that I should clear my desk immediately and leave the premises! Suddenly I was out of a job and there seemed nothing I could do to change to situation. It was difficult to break the news to my wife, who was at home looking after our three small children. I was the only breadwinner, but I had now lost the means to provide for any of our needs. I encouraged myself by bringing to mind the scriptures where God promises to supply the needs of those who put their trust in Him.

For a while I think I was in shock, but then after thinking the whole situation through for a period of time I came to the conclusion that I had no other option but to try and defend my actions. A friend of mine who I had shared my problem with agreed with me and summed it up this way:

"As I see it, Trev, if they can do this kind of thing to you, they can do it to anyone. By defending your own position you are probably helping someone else further down the line."

I could see the logic in that and I figured that the best way for me to make a protest was to go to a tribunal for religious discrimination. However, finding a solicitor proved to be incredibly difficult. Each one that I approached told me that I did not have a strong enough case, although given the circumstances I felt sure that I did. Eventually a Christian working at a local law centre in the town where I live told me that he thought I did have a strong enough case to be considered and offered to help me prepare for the tribunal.

It took quite a bit of time to put the case together, but in the end I didn't need his help because the organisation that gave me the sack heard what I was planning to do and offered to pay an out of court settlement to me, which after a lot of heart searching I reluctantly accepted.

Although that seemed to sort things out in a fairly unsatisfactory way, my problems were not at an end. Because I had been dismissed from my job, I found it difficult to get new work, which was very worrying, because I had a wife and family to support. I kept wondering if I had been right in accepting the out of court settlement. I was far from sure that I had done the right thing. But then I had to remind myself that all those who I had asked for advice, including my friends at church, told me that I should take the money that had been offered, but I still feel that in some ways I compromised my faith by doing so.

I found it very difficult to lose a job that I had felt dedicated to and was doing well in. I guess the management found it easy to get rid of me because I was still working through my probationary period. The other Christian that took a stand with me had a difficult time in a different way. She did not lose her job, probably because she had been working for the organisation longer than I had, but they still made it very hard for her. She was taken into several meetings where she was shouted at and her Christian faith was ridiculed. In spite of all that she stood by all that she believed, but I know she found it a very gruelling time, sometimes leaving the meetings in tears.

When I lost my job I had no idea how long it would be before I would be able to get another one. Some days my wife and I did not know where the next penny would come from to provide for ourselves and our three children. However, God always did provide, often through members of our church who were nudged by the Lord to help us at strategic times.

I am now working happily as a primary school teacher and in some ways what I had to endure is now fading as a distant memory. But there is part of me that cannot forget how, as a born-again believer, I was humiliated by a Christian organisation just because I would not participate in a festival to a foreign god. I still believe that if Christianity is worth anything, it's worth standing up for. I'm proud to be a follower of Jesus and no loss of job or earnings can compare to what I have as a believer in Him.

All Who Live Godly Lives...

Eric Forde was a miner who knew how to do a hard day's work for a fair day's pay. It was a Billy Graham meeting which put him on the Christian road that eventually found him as vicar of a church in a predominately Muslim neighbourhood. Eric knew he had taken on a tough assignment, but it wasn't until he saw Asian young men entering his church through a hole in the door that they had made, with petrol cans in their hands that he realised just how tough it had become...

I come from a working-class background and I'm proud of my roots. I was brought up in a mining community and when the time came for me to leave school and find employment, like many of my classmates, I found work down the mines. The work was hard and dirty, but honest. I knew what I had achieved at the end of each shift. The job kept me in touch with reality.

As a child though, my parents had always told me about another kind of reality, the kind that can't be touched or handled or tasted. They were both God-fearing people who went to church each Sunday. I didn't reject what they told me, but I knew that what they believed was not real in my own life, so although I went along to church each Sunday as a child,

I didn't experience anything special or supernatural during those Sunday mornings filled with hymns and prayers and sermons. And although I didn't know it then, in my mid twenties, things were going to dramatically change.

The month was June and I was in bed with flu. Before I had fallen ill with an aching head and joints, things had been going well. I had married Elsie, the girl I had been engaged to for a couple of years, and we had moved into our first home together. But the flu bug had stopped me in my tracks and all I could do was stare at the ceiling and wait for the bug to take its course.

Suddenly I heard a knock at the front door and my wife talking to someone. The next thing I knew she was showing the caller into my bedroom. I recognised the voice before its owner entered the room. It was Miss Sparrowhawk. Now in her mid 70s, everyone in the village knew her for her kind deeds and generosity. If anyone was in need she would be the first to call round with an offer of help. She attended the Anglican Church in the morning and the Methodist Chapel in the evening, but wore her faith very lightly and was accepted and loved by everyone who came into contact with her. Her face creased into a smile when she saw me and her grey eyes twinkled.

"Hello, Eric. I heard that you weren't well. I've just brought you some fruit and a few magazines to cheer you up a little." She hesitated for a second before continuing. "But that's not the real reason for coming to see you, I must admit. God has been talking directly to me – about you! And He gave me a message for you. Please listen carefully."

I didn't know whether to laugh or hide under the bed-clothes in panic. But there was such an earnest look in her eyes, I knew that what she wanted to say was important. Miss Sparrowhawk had a genuinely close walk with God, everyone knew that.

She said that the American evangelist, Billy Graham, was coming to England and that God that told her that I must attend. She had been trying to fill a coach to take people there, with little success. Now God had told her that I must go – and before I could go, I must persuade enough people to fill the coach to come with me!

As odd as the message sounded I knew in some instinctive way that it was God speaking through her. So, as soon as I was well I started to tell all the people I knew what I had heard about Billy Graham, which wasn't much, and why they should go and hear him speak. It was hard going, but in the end somehow or other I managed to fill the coach with people, in spite of the fact that some were not initially all that keen. Miss Sparrowhawk told me that she had been sent tickets through the post and on the evening in question, with my wife beside me, we all set off to hear Billy Graham speak.

The coach was later setting off than I had planned. Some people had found it a bit of a dash to finish work, get changed and then get to the coach by the agreed time. When we arrived at the football stadium where Dr Graham was due to speak, we saw hundreds of other coaches, all full, with many people thronging through the gates. I heaved a sigh of relief that we had tickets, only to discover when we presented them at one of the gates that they weren't tickets of admission, but just leaflets advertising the venue! I felt pretty fed up. Every gate I went to was closed – there was no way any of us was going to get into the stadium. I wondered just what God was up to. He had told me to come and had even said that I had to bring a coach load of people with me. I had done all of that and now I couldn't even see the man I had come to hear, although I did note that there was a large screen outside the stadium to accommodate those who were left outside.

I turned round to find out what my wife made of it all, only to realise that in the crush I had lost her. My evening was rapidly going downhill. In spite of the fact that I had no real relationship with God, I started to speak to Him. "I just don't understand what is going on. Why would You bring me all this way, just to stand outside a stadium, especially when I've done everything You asked me to do? I can't work it out."

I closed my eyes, more in frustration than prayer, trying to come to a place of peace in all that was going on. Then the most unusual thing happened. It was as though I started to be transported right into the stadium and on to the platform, ending up standing directly in front of Billy Graham as he started to speak! I didn't know what to make of it all and kept my eyes firmly shut. The message that he began to deliver could have been prepared especially for me. It was all to do with Abraham and how he was willing to sacrifice his son Isaac. "What are you willing to sacrifice to follow God?" Dr Graham challenged. "God wants you. He wants you to surrender everything into His hands and to ask Jesus into your life."

I knew that what God was demanding of me was very costly, but that I must respond to the message I had heard. I bowed my head and asked Jesus to come and live in my heart. I then opened my eyes, to discover that I was standing outside the stadium, just as I had been before I closed my eyes.

My wife was still nowhere to be seen and I went in search of her. Within a short space of time we were reunited and I tried to explain to her what I had experienced. Like me, she had been deeply moved by the message and told me that she too had asked Jesus into her heart and life. Getting on our knees, with people walking all around us, we held hands and prayed together for God to use us in whatever way He could. We went back on the coach that night two very different people from the ones that had set off several hours before.

It wasn't long before my mining days were behind me and I started on the long road to becoming a vicar in the Church of England. Eventually I ended up in a parish which at one time had been a thriving working-class community, but by the time I arrived had changed into one where around 98% of the people in the parish were of Asian origin, many of whom were Muslim.

That was a challenge, of course, but not one that I wanted to shy away from. I knew that God never told anyone to be successful, just faithful and obedient, and I wanted to be both. The church I had been called to was made up of people of mixed race, some white, some Caribbean and one or two from Pakistan. They were various ages too, some who were single, but also a good number of families who saw this church as their spiritual home. We also had various groups meeting at the church on a weekly basis including a small but dedicated Ladies Group and an enthusiastic Brownie Pack.

When I first arrived, relationships with the local Muslim population were not great, but reasonable. They didn't really want anything to do with us socially, but appeared to accept our presence in the community, partly I suppose because the church had been there when they first arrived. But that attitude started to change over the next couple of years as incidents like 9/11 began to occur. The youth in the area became more disaffected. I was told that the teaching in the mosques became more radical and racial tensions began to be heightened too.

Just across the road from the church was a piece of waste ground. Each November the local youth would build a bonfire there. As the 5th of November approached I noticed wood being brought to the ground each day and made a mental note to offer the lads a tree that one of my church wardens had chopped down a couple of weeks before at the back of the church.

As I drove up to the church a few days before Bonfire Night, hoping to talk to someone I could offer the wood to, I was horrified to see that some of the young men were lighting rockets and then aiming them at people walking on the pavement, some of which were mothers with small children! What they were doing was incredibly dangerous and I couldn't believe what I was seeing. I also noticed that although the big bonfire was still waiting to be lit, a series of smaller bonfires were burning, some of which looked as though they were getting out of control.

As I wondered what action to take the Fire Service arrived, probably alerted by one of the residents who lived nearby. The firemen made short work of the bonfires, but I was later to discover that they had drenched the fireworks as well, making the youngsters very angry. I drove off to check the back of the church and was only away from the scene a few minutes. When I returned I saw seven or eight Muslim young men going up the steps of the church and into the building. I knew that none of my people were scheduled to be in the church at that point, that there was no service that evening, and therefore the church should not have been able to have been accessed by anyone. Then, as I got nearer to the building I could see how access had been made possible. Someone had hacked a big hole in the church door and some of Asian youth that had been lighting fires across the road were now going inside the church with petrol cans in their hands.

I knew I had to act quickly and that I couldn't deal with this situation on my own. I drove round the corner to make a call to the Police on my mobile. As I was in the process of doing that, I suddenly realised that my car had been surrounded by a very angry group of Asian young men. One of them picked up a large stone and threw it at the back window of the car which instantly shattered, as he shouted, "Take that, you white bastard."

I put my foot down on the accelerator and drove round the corner again to the church and to my relief I discovered that the Police had arrived. The young men that had entered the church had run off when they realised that the Police were on the scene. I, along with the two policemen, pushed past the barricade that they had made and saw what they had been busy doing.

Bibles and hymnbooks had been thrown onto the floor and then petrol poured on them. There were rockets pointing at various parts of the church, ready to be set alight, and petrol had also been poured on the pews and the carpet. The crazy thing was that they had initially barricaded the door that they had entered by, obviously thinking that they would make good their escape by a door at the back of the church. They had no way of knowing that this door was double locked in three places and it would have been impossible for them to have escaped from that exit. In short, they would have all been burnt alive if we had not turned up when we did, cutting short their plans to set the church alight. What started as an act of vandalism could have ended up with several young men being burnt to death. It just doesn't bear thinking about.

No one was ever brought to book for the damage to the church building and once things had calmed down a little we did what we could to reach out once more to the Muslim community, but with very little response.

For a few weeks an uneasy peace prevailed, but it wasn't long before members of the Ladies Group were being threatened as they made their way to church for their weekly Thursday evening meeting. I suggested that they might want to consider changing the time of the meeting to an afternoon, so that they would be safer. But they wouldn't hear of it. "We have met on a Thursday evening at 8 o'clock for the last twenty years, to pray and give thanks to God, and we're not going to stop now for anyone," I was told. I admired their spirit. I did become concerned though when the Brownies started to be pelted with eggs and spat upon as they made their way to the church. The mosques in our area were, by all accounts, preaching a very hard and uncompromising message against Christians, which was having an effect on the young people of the area, many of which came from poor backgrounds with little or no chance of work.

I believed that it was no accident that our church building was placed where it was, in the very centre of what was now a very Muslim populated area. I knew that the strongest

weapon that we had to fight what was happening to us as
a church was prayer – and love for those who hated us.
I decided to set up a prayer meeting every week day at noon. I
was amazed and heartened to see how many members of the
church wanted to be there as often as they could make it. It
started to be a vital part of the church's activities and the Holy
Spirit began to speak words of encouragement to us all. On
one memorable day, when several church members had
suffered quite a bit at the hands of those hostile to them
because of their faith in Jesus, the Lord spoke in prophecy as
we were waiting upon Him. This is what He said:

> "If you were not doing My work, you would not be persecuted.
> The devil does not persecute churches that are not working for
> Me. What you need to know is that I am protecting you."

As I heard what was being said, I was reminded of one of the
promises in the Bible that nobody likes to recall, and not
many, if any, have put music to. It is found in 2 Timothy 3:12.
In the Revised Standard Version it reads:

> "Indeed all who desire to live a godly life in Christ Jesus will be
> persecuted."

We tried once more to reach out to the Muslim community,
but with little success. And still the attacks occurred, with fires
started outside the church, gates and walls destroyed and
members of the congregation abused. When the church was
doused in petrol on that November afternoon some expected
us to shut up shop and move to another location. But none of
our church members felt we should do that. We believed then
and continue to believe that God wants a Christian witness in
this area. And instead of people leaving the church in fear of
what has gone on, church numbers have actually grown! We
are paying a price, but the reward is a new vitality and

freedom in worship. We don't just believe that God is with us – we know He is!

Not all of our neighbours feel hostile towards us. In fact, on one or two occasions it has been members of the Asian community that have reported incidents to the Police that they have seen which have been directed against the church. And the problem is not exclusively ours – occasionally a mosque gets targeted by yobs, just like we do.

The facts are, though, that hurting people often hurt others! If we were to seek to take revenge it would immediately spoil our witness and give the wrong image of the loving God that we serve. He is giving us the strength day by day to show the love of God to all those that we live and worship amongst, and we know that love is the strongest thing that we can display to this community that so needs to know the true love of God in their lives.

A Love to Die For?

In spite of the fact that her parents were both dedicated Muslims, Treena was sent to a Church of England school where her teacher told her class stories of Jesus. Her conversion to Christianity was just about tolerated by her parents, who thought it was a phase that would pass, but when, as a sixteen year old she wanted to get baptised she was forced into hiding to avoid the wrath of her parents and to evade marrying a man they had chosen for her. It was at that point that death threats started to become something she could not ignore...

I've always thought of myself as British. I was, after all, born in England, and have always lived here. What was different about me compared to most of my school friends was that my parents were from Turkey and still had strong links with the country in spite of the fact that they had lived in England for almost twenty years. They were both practising Muslims – in fact my father was an Imam in the mosque in the middle of the town that I grew up in. So from a very young age I was taught all about Islam, its rules and customs.

However, in spite of the fact that Islam touched every part of our lives, my parents were both realistic enough to understand that when I got to school age I needed to get a good basic education. The local primary school had an excellent reputation and so once I was old enough my parents made arrangements for me to attend there. I am not sure whether they even realised it or not, but it was a Church of England primary school, which meant that all my class were told stories about Jesus. And that is all that they were to me at the time – nice stories about Jesus, who Muslims recognise as a prophet – and it's true to say a very important prophet, but no more than that.

At the age of eleven I left that school and started my secondary education. Like the rest of my school friends it was a big step in my life and a lot of what I had learned about Jesus faded into the background as I studied hard in key subjects to get good exam results. However, God really must have been looking over my life because my Religious Education teacher in my last year at school was a born-again Christian and it was through her that I eventually came to faith in Jesus. She explained in a very straightforward fashion the way of salvation, telling me that I could have a place in heaven not because I had lived a good life, because nobody could live a life good enough to get into heaven, but only if I believed that Jesus died on the Cross for *me* and when He hung there He was dealing with *my* sins, and that I believed that He was therefore *my* Saviour.

There was quite a lot of tension in my home which made me feel unhappy. Mum and Dad didn't see eye to eye all the time. That was just one of many reasons why I wanted the happiness that my teacher talked about. But I knew enough about Islam to know that it was totally forbidden for a Muslim to become a believer in Jesus. I thought long and hard about what I should do – it was not a quick decision. Then, one New Year's Day I decided that I wanted to ask Jesus into my heart. After I had taken that step I felt so happy – a new year and a new start.

The way Jesus started to change my life and my attitude to

life must have been obvious to those around me, because before too long my parents found out what I had done. I think they thought it was some kind of rebellious gesture that I would grow out of and to my surprise and relief nothing much was said.

However, when I told them that I wanted to get baptised everything changed very quickly. My dad was furious. He told me that getting baptised was out of the question for me because he had arranged for someone to marry me – and that I had no choice in the matter.

I stared at him in disbelief. I couldn't believe what was being said. Who was this man that they wanted me to marry? When was I supposed to be getting married? Did I not get a say in what was being planned, I wanted to know.

My father hit the roof! "Don't you talk to me like that! You are only sixteen remember."

"Yes, I know," I said in tears, "and as far as I'm concerned I'm not ready to marry anyone at the moment – can't you see that?"

My mother stood in the corner of the room, not saying anything but obviously very upset. They had both obviously hoped that I would just agree to what they were planning. Maybe if I hadn't had the kind of Western education that they had provided for me, I might have seen things differently. But as much as I loved them, I couldn't go ahead with their arrangements. Every time the subject was brought up after that, a row started, and in the end I decided to run away. I found somewhere to live and hoped that I would not be found. But it was a vain hope. My father discovered where I had moved to and made plans to make me come home and renounce my faith in Jesus.

I was alone in the house on the day that my father decided to do something about me, his rebellious daughter. Although I was alone he most certainly was not. In fact he arrived with about fifty other men, all intent on "persuading" me to do what he wanted – which was to renounce my faith in Jesus, return home and get married!

The first I knew that I had been discovered was when my father began banging on the door, demanding to be let in. Just the tone of his voice told me that it would be unwise to do what he was asking! I peered cautiously through an upstairs window and saw not just my dad but the men he had brought with him. When I refused to open the door the banging started to get louder and it soon became clear that they were trying to break the door down, while others were banging on the windows. What defence did I have against so many men? Why did they have to come when I was completely alone in the house? I knew it would be several hours before any of my house mates were due to return. I felt very alone. The odds were completely stacked against me.

Then I suddenly remembered something that Jesus had said which I had read in the Bible a few days before. I couldn't remember it word for word, but it was something about never leaving those that He loved on their own, but sending the Holy Spirit to help them. I wasn't sure if I could immediately find it in the Bible, but I knew it was there somewhere. In any case, I didn't have time to look it up, I just needed to see it outworked in this situation. While the noise outside the house continued, I started to pray.

"Jesus, You know how scared I am right now. Any moment that door could burst open and if that happened, I am not sure what those men would do to me – they sound so angry. I'm asking You to protect me and save me in this situation in whatever way You see fit."

The hammering on the door continued for a few moments more, then I began to realise that it was no longer as intense as it had been at the beginning. It sounded as though they were getting tired, losing interest, whatever. I screwed up all my courage and peeked out of the window again, this time to see some of them walking down the drive and getting into cars.

Within the next five minutes they had all left, including my dad, and I was alone again and completely unharmed. I still don't understand how God caused all the men to give up and leave me alone. To me, it was nothing short of a miracle.

I knew, however, that the matter would not end there. Now that they had tried and failed to get me to return home, at some point in the future they would be back. When my house mates returned, I told them in tears that I would have to move. It was no longer safe for me to live there and if I remained it would also put their lives in danger too.

Within twenty-four hours I had found a new place to stay and that began a pattern, which I still adopt, of moving house every few months and giving my address to only a very few hand-chosen friends. Since the day when my father and his supporters came to try and get me I have received many death threats, all of which I take seriously. I have learnt not to use the same routes back and forth from home and to alter the times that I do things as much as I can.

My relationship with Jesus had become wonderful and very precious, but I no longer had any kind of relationship with my own family. This made me feel very sad, but I could not deny my growing faith. It was worth everything that I had to go through. But I can understand very well why Muslims do not readily become Christians. The cost is very high – and can sometimes result in them losing their lives. There are many Islamic communities within the British Isles, tight-knit communities where family honour is very prominent. If a person within that community converts to Christianity it is looked upon as a very shameful thing and sometimes death is the only way that the family's honour can be restored.

Now I spend my time speaking to teenagers about my faith and how becoming a Christian is a life-changing experience which will have an eternal impact. I've had the privilege of leading several girls to the Lord, all from a Muslim background. Understandably, none of them feel that they can speak openly about their faith, so they meet secretly together to read the Bible and to pray. It is very difficult for people from other faith backgrounds to become Christians, because of the pressures that are brought to bear on anyone who wants to take that route. Very often, the Christian community is totally unaware of the pressures that young converts from other faith backgrounds have and therefore they fail to give them the help and support that they so desperately need.

Although I was in no way ready to get married at sixteen, especially to someone I didn't know and who didn't share my Christian faith, I would of course love to get married one day and start to live some kind of normal life. But I'm not complaining. I have always had people from the family of God to help me when I've needed it and knowing Jesus is the greatest thing that anyone can ever experience.

Do you love Jesus? Enough to die for Him? That is the question that many Muslims have to ask themselves before opening up their hearts to Him. That is the dilemma that many face in the United Kingdom today.

CHAPTER 7

Christianity under the Microscope

Sami was born in Egypt. His driving passion was to be a world famous scientist. Then, following a terrible road accident he heard the claims of Jesus, which ultimately changed the course of his life. But before giving his life to Jesus he knew he had to do an exhaustive study of both the Qur'an and the Bible to find out for himself what each book had to say about life and eternity. All his energies are now directed towards bringing others to faith in God. Sometimes he does so at risk to his own personal safety, even though he is based in the UK...

There was always something about the sea that fascinated me. Egypt gets very hot in the summer, so I used to love it when my parents took me to the coast. I would watch the waves crashing onto the shore, wondering what lay beyond the horizon. I also used to wonder what kind of creatures lived in the ocean depths, which to me as a child seemed so mysterious. As I sat by the ocean, enjoying the sound of the sea and the movement of the waves, I used to speculate about all kinds of things. What was life all about? Why were we here? There seemed to be no answer to so many of my questions.

My parents were Muslims and brought me up to read the Qur'an. As I grew, it seemed to offer few answers to the questions I had about life. In my search for a key to the things that puzzled me, I would occasionally read the Bible, but I found it difficult to understand and I was always fearful that I would get into trouble if someone discovered me reading what was, in my culture, a forbidden book.

After leaving school I went to university to study biology. I hadn't been there long before news reached me that my older brother had become a Christian, bringing great shame on our Muslim family. I wanted to find out why he had taken such a drastic step, but did not know where I could contact him as he had been forced to leave home after his conversion to the Christian faith.

I enjoyed life at the university. I worked hard and made many new friends. It was wonderful to be in an atmosphere where people were thirsty for knowledge and were searching for truth in whatever subject they were studying.

Every morning I used to cycle to university, enjoying the short ten minute ride which kept me fit and allowed me to think through the day whilst I was travelling along. I got to the point where I knew the route very well and could almost make the journey with my eyes closed. Then one morning when I *had* to close my eyes just for a second to avoid the strong morning sun, a car came out of nowhere and threw me off my bike, causing me to fall under the vehicle. I could hear a lot of noise and the shouts of people as they endeavoured to rescue me. I felt bruised and shaken up, but what bothered me most was that my right eye was hurting and I couldn't see anything.

I was rushed to the hospital and after being examined by the doctor he informed me that I had no broken bones, but that I was going to lose the sight of my right eye, and that there was nothing he could do to save it. I felt absolutely devastated. I lay in my hospital bed with my eye heavily bandaged, wondering how my life would be from now on and how I was going to cope.

A few days later, to my surprise, a nurse came and told me that I had a visitor. As soon as my visitor started to speak I knew who it was. It was my brother who had become a Christian a couple of years before. After we had caught up with each other's news, he started to tell me the difference that Jesus had made in his life and how much Jesus loves all those who put their trust in Him.

"Listen, Sami," he said, "there are some great doctors in this hospital I'm sure, but Jesus is the greatest doctor that has ever lived. Put your trust in Him, you will never regret it. Come on, let's pray together."

We started to pray and I prayed that if Jesus healed my eye, I would serve Him for the rest of my life. After my brother left the hospital, I asked my doctor if he would remove the bandages that were over my damaged eye. At first he refused, but when I continued to ask for this to be done he finally agreed. Slowly and carefully he carried out his task and when all the bandages had gone he was astonished to discover that I could see perfectly well! A miracle had occurred.

Shortly after that amazing incident I was discharged from hospital, but I soon forgot all about the promises that I had made to Jesus to serve Him if He healed me. Instead I just carried on with my studies, eventually leaving Egypt after gaining a degree, making a new life for myself in Sri Lanka. I was now a well respected Marine Biologist, making some pretty significant discoveries. I became the first person to find and log four previously unknown sea plants. And yet, in spite of all my success, there was an emptiness inside. I began to realise that although I had made some major discoveries in my chosen profession I also needed to investigate the claims of both the Muslim and Christian faiths. It was then that I decided to carry out a comparative study into what both religions said about themselves, to see how they stacked up against each other. I knew that Islam says that people can never be sure that their sins are forgiven, whilst Christianity says the complete opposite. I was now on a mission to discover which one was true. Each evening after work I would pore over books on the two faiths. I wanted to find out as much as I could about each one of them. In the end it became clear to me that it was only by having a personal trust in Jesus that our sins could be dealt with, through His death on the Cross, and His resurrection. At the end of my search I knew that if I wanted to follow the truth I would need to become a follower of Jesus who said that He *was* the way, the truth and the life. This was not an easy decision to make – I knew it would begin to affect every part of my life from that moment on.

Although I'd had great success in my career as a Marine Biologist, I knew that I needed to continue to study my new found faith. Soon I was enrolling in a four-year theology course, at the end of which I gained an MA. But what was important was not the letters I now had after my name, but the relationship I now had with Jesus. I wanted to share with as many people as I could the things that I had discovered. I prayed long and hard as to where the Lord Jesus wanted me to go to start my work for Him and eventually I was lead to go to live and work in Manchester.

The streets of Manchester were very different from those that I had known up until then. The sights and smells were different and when I looked up no longer were there blue skies, but often the sky was grey and overcast. But I had the Son – God's Son – in my heart, and although I was sad to leave my work as a scientist, I knew that I was on the path that God had called me to. The big question was, how to reach the people who needed to hear the message of salvation in such a big city? I had no idea. Then one day I saw that someone had set up a table on one of the wide pavements in Manchester and was selling some craft items that they had made. I wondered if I could do the same, but instead of craft items, put Christian books for people to look at and buy. At least the books would be a way of opening up conversations with people as they went by, I thought.

So this is what I did and I was surprised to discover how many did stop and want to talk to me about the books I had on display. I still do that today. I think that many who stop and talk would not do so if I was in a shop somewhere, but because I am there as they walk by, I believe they find it easy to relate to me. When I first started doing this kind of work things sometimes became tense if Muslims who came to look at what I had on the stall realised that I had once been a Muslim too, but mainly it was OK. Then the Twin Towers outrage occurred in New York and the mood seemed to change overnight. Suddenly Muslims became much more threatening and abusive when they saw what I was doing.

By this time I not only had the book table on the pavement, but I had started to speak in churches and at public meetings, as well as operating a website. All these things allowed me to speak to a much wider public than my little bookstall on the pavement did. However, with the greater exposure came the greater danger. At one meeting I was involved in a while ago, after I had spoken, I was surrounded by a mob of between seventy and eighty people and the Police had to be called. It was a very tense situation, but I believed that God would protect me, and He did. I have to say that I was not put off by that incident. I continue to speak in public halls and churches, mainly in the Manchester area, but I'm realistic about the dangers that speaking publicly poses.

It is not unusual for me to have death threats on my life and I know the people who make these threats are not just playing around with words. Some of the more radical ones have been taught to hate the message that the Bible teaches, but in spite of that I feel that I must continue the work that God has given me to do. It is too important for me to neglect and for those listening to ignore.

Sometimes I wonder what life might have been like had I

not had that accident, which seemed to be the worst thing that had happened to me at the time, but proved to be the way that God was able to grab my attention and allow me to not only to hear about His love for me, but to experience it too, when my eye was dramatically healed. I am so grateful to my brother who took the time to come and pray for me and that God has given me the courage to explain the wonderful news that Jesus came so that all who believed in Him could be saved from their sins, and live with Him throughout eternity.

How long will I be able to do the kind of work that I am doing on the streets and in the public halls in Britain? I am not sure. More and more, people who preach the Gospel are looked at as those who are rocking the boat in society and causing "unnecessary tensions". But what could be more important than where people will spend eternity?

Sometimes when I was a child on a visit to the coast I would look out to sea and the water would be calm. On other occasions, the seas would be rough and angry. That is now how my life has become. Sometimes when I preach the Gospel it is received with gentleness in a calm atmosphere. On other occasions, elements within the crowd try and whip up a storm. But I know the One who calms the angry wind and waves and as long as I stay close to Him, I know I will be safe.

Some people have said to me, "What if the Bible is wrong about Jesus and He is not the Son of God? You have thrown away a good career as a scientist to follow a religion that is false." But I say to them, "What if I am right and what the Bible claims is absolutely true – that Jesus is the Son of God and there is no way to heaven but through Him? That then means that all who have failed to put their trust in Him go to a lost eternity. Could any message be more important than that, and could any career be more important than telling others how to gain eternal life? I don't think so."

Backchat

Marian had a nice job in a pleasant school in a beautiful part of England, the last place you would expect people to object to Christians or the Christian way of life. But in contrast to the lovely surroundings in which she lived and worked, there was a dark and ugly attitude by some of the staff towards her, and by just living out her Christian life she seemed to provoke the most unpleasant reactions from fellow staff members. Then she discovered that without a doubt God knew what she was experiencing. This is her story.

There was hardly a time when I was not aware of God's love in my life. It's not that I came from a particularly strong Christian family, although both my parents were believers. It's just that for some reason or other I have always seemed to be aware of spiritual things. For instance, when I was told at the age of four that my great aunt had died, I had a clear picture in my mind of her going to heaven although no one had talked to me about such things.

I started to attend primary school when I was five. Unlike many children today I had no pre-school build up, so before the first day dawned I became increasingly apprehensive every time I thought about having to go to school, because I didn't know what would be expected of me. Once I was there, of course, I started to realise that it wasn't so bad after all and I began to settle down.

One of the lessons that we had each week was Physical Education. It was held in what seemed to me like a very big hall. On one of the walls was a coloured print of Jesus reproduced, I think, from some painting that had been created by an artist years before. Although there was nothing particularly special about this picture, every time I went past it I would stop and stare at it, and each time I did, I felt Jesus' love for me. It was just a wonderful thing that God allowed me to experience, especially as I never went to Sunday school, because the church my parents went to, which I didn't set foot in until I was around the age of nine, was a very formal Anglican church which didn't cater for young children. But I was fortunate enough to have a school teacher who told my class Bible stories in such a way that the characters seemed to come alive. By the time I was twelve I had been confirmed and although my spiritual journey has had its ups and downs, since the spiritual renewal that I experienced about ten years ago I have enjoyed a strong relationship with God.

I married in my early twenties to a Christian man and we have two wonderful teenage children who are also believers. We live in a very pleasant part of England and although I have had various jobs during my working life, I am at present a teaching assistant at a primary school. There are no real problems or tensions in the school – it's just not that kind of area. There are virtually no children from an ethnic minority background, so it seemed reasonable to assume that living out a Christian life in such an environment would be easy. But I began to discover that just under the surface of what appeared to be a respectable Christian environment were attitudes and thoughts which were far from Christian. Let me explain.

Although I was enjoying my work with the children I had responsibility for, which often meant coming alongside them and giving them the confidence they needed if they had fallen behind with their work, I started to be aware of a rather negative attitude in the staff room, which was often quite mocking towards Christianity. It was frequently generated by those who went in for heavy drinking, who would look down on those who preferred not to join in, labelling them as "not one of the crowd". As far as I am concerned, I have nothing against alcohol as such, and quite happily go to a pub for a meal with my friends from time to time. But I don't particularly want to be around when people start behaving inappropriately and unprofessionally, so I tend to avoid those kinds of gatherings if at all possible.

Every academic year, Teaching Assistants are allocated to work with a designated teacher and are informed of this allocation in the summer term of the previous year. I discovered that I had been allocated to work with a male teacher who I had worked with previously. As far as I was concerned we had a friendly professional relationship – in fact, he often praised my efforts with the children in my care.

However, one day when I left the room for a short time while this male teacher was training some Teaching Assistants, one of them, who I had noticed tended to ignore me or treat me with distain and who also had a hostile attitude towards Christianity, asked the teacher who he would be working with during the next term. When he said my name, nobody spoke, and he said with a smirk,

"The silence says it all." This provoked much laughter. Then he said, "Oh well, I'll have to mind my Ps and Qs. No more swearing." This was all said in the presence of a friend of mine who was not a Christian at the time, but became a believer a little while later. Sadly this was not an isolated incident, but because nothing was said to me directly to my face and I did not learn about it all until some considerable time later, I couldn't really confront anyone or come to my own defence.

So I suppose the next thing is to ask oneself why people act the way that they do towards me and other members of staff who are practising Christians. I don't actually think that there is one definitive answer to that. I do, however, believe that some of the teachers are under conviction. For instance, one teacher in the school gets very angry every time she has to teach a class about religious studies, saying to anyone who will listen to her in the staff room how she loathes Bible stories, referring to them as "rubbish". Another one bizarrely makes constant reference to Christianity in whatever subject or conversation he is taking part in, and then glances in my direction to see my reaction. And if he swears and then realises I'm around he makes the biggest fuss in offering an apology. The thing is that having been involved in prison visiting which our church has organised over the years, I've probably heard more swear words that he has! I am not easily shocked – what real Christian is? – and when I hear persistent profanity coming from the lips of the teaching assistant who is hostile towards me and the Christian faith, I take it as a reminder to thank Jesus for all that He has done for me. Maybe it is that non-Christian people recognise that the Holy Spirit is living in those who have accepted Jesus into their lives more than the Christians themselves do!

In spite of the fact that I have found that Christianity is mocked and individual Christians reviled, the interesting thing is that sometimes when things go badly wrong for someone, it is often a Christian that is sought out to offer comfort and sympathy. The event that I am going to tell you about illustrates that point.

Sometime after the unpleasant incident when I was laughed at behind my back, I was in a country pub one lunchtime enjoying a meal with a friend. Suddenly one of the male teachers who I knew to be particularly hostile to what I believed burst through the doors looking quite distraught. His look quickly turned to surprise when he saw me sitting there.

Probably a pub was the last place he thought he would find me in! Instead of avoiding me, which I thought would be his reaction, he made a bee-line to my table and asked if he could chat to me for a few moments.

He then started to tell me how he had just returned from an interview for a job that he really wanted and had put in a lot of preparation for, only to be told that he had he had been unsuccessful. Of course, I listened sympathetically, then reminded him of all the things that he had in his favour, which would, I felt sure, eventually get him the job he wanted. He seemed helped by what I was able to say and grateful to be able to talk to someone who was prepared to offer a listening ear. That was on the Friday. But sadly, by the Monday he was back in the staff room talking about "religious people" in a very disparaging way.

I keep a spiritual journal and so I know that around this time I was reading *The Heavenly Man* by Brother Yun. I found all that this wonderful Chinese Christian had to endure very difficult to read. I couldn't begin to think how I might cope given the sort of circumstances he went through. The only way I found it possible to read the book was by reading it a little at a time, so it was a while before I finished it. Towards the end of the book, Brother Yun said that he believed that Christians in the West would increasingly experience ridicule, slander and rejection. I put the book down after reading that statement and thought, "I'm not experiencing anything like that in my life," but then within a few days the incident where I was talked and laughed about behind my back had happened.

However, God knows and sees all. And sometimes He goes out of His way to let us know that simple fact. About a month after all this had happened I attended a meeting that had been organised by my church. One of the speakers was an American preacher who, at the end of his talk, invited those who wanted prayer to come forward. Along with several others I went out to the front of the church to be prayed for by his man who had never met me and therefore knew absolutely nothing about me. I was asking for prayer on a totally unconnected issue to the one that was going on at work and I didn't mention that situation to him at all, and yet as he prayed for me he suddenly said that there was something in my background – he stopped for a moment and then said "persecution" and continued, saying that I was being mocked and ridiculed for my faith, that I could not convince or change the attitude of the people behind this, but I just had to pray for them. This man could not have known anything about what I had experienced – very few people did, so I knew that it was God telling me that He knew and was there to help me.

How do Christians in the West fight the kind of persecution that comes our way? Not with tanks, bombs and bullets that's for sure. The apostle Paul tells us in 2 Corinthians 10 that,

> "... the weapons of our warfare are not carnal, but mighty through God to the pulling down of strong holds; casting down imaginations, and every high thing that exalteth itself against the knowledge of God, and bringing into captivity every thought to the obedience of Christ."   (vv. 4–5 KJV).

Love is the answer. It is the most powerful "weapon" that we Christians have at our disposal. Ultimately it will crack open the hardest heart as we endeavour to show the love of God to those that we come into contact with in an increasingly cynical and loveless world.

A Brush with the Law

Raymond is no bigoted Bible punching sectarian with a religious axe to grind. He is in fact a wonderfully happy family man, a trained accountant now in his seventies who loves the Lord and wants everyone to know how much God loves them. His relationship with God was so wonderful that he wanted to share it with as many people as he could, so he thought of a simple and effective way of doing just that. But he was shocked when he was stopped and questioned by the Police at a mainline train station, just because he had a placard around his neck saying "Jesus is Lord". This is his story.

Some people can quote the year, month, day and hour when they gave their lives to the Lord. It's not like that with me. I grew slowly into the Christian life – but I know I'm saved! God has been really good to me and I've felt His hand of blessing on me all my life.

I was born in Africa over seventy years ago. Were my family Christians? Yes and no! Culturally they were, but neither Dad nor Mum had a real relationship with the Almighty, although having said that I remember Mum praying to God a lot when I was a boy, so maybe there was more going on in her spiritual life than I ever knew.

When I was old enough to begin my education I started to attend a school run by the Salvation Army. They were good people, but they were very strict. They wanted us all to work hard and get a good education. There was nothing hi-tech about our schoolroom. We were given sticks of chalk to write with on slates, so if we made a mistake, we just rubbed it out and started again. I was happy at that school and life was good. Sadly though, I had to leave quite suddenly. You see, my father was a miner and worked long hours in difficult conditions. One day I returned home to discover that Dad had been involved in an accident in the mine. He was not killed, but the injuries he sustained meant that he could no longer work there any more. Soon we were on the move to a different part of Africa and eventually I started to attend a new school.

My new school was run by Scottish missionaries. Like those at my old school, my new teachers also wanted to give all the students a good education. The school maintained high standards, so my parents were happy for me to attend, but the journey I undertook each day was fairly hazardous. There were no cars or motorbikes that could be a danger to me, but the threat came from things far more deadly. In order to get from my house to the school I had to walk through an area where lions, hyena and flying snakes lived. I was always glad when I made it safely to school. Strangely enough though, it was a creature that one could hardly see with the human eye that became a threat to my health. It was a cattle tic that did not live in the part of Africa that I had originally come from, so I guess I was vulnerable to it. And sure enough, I came down with a terrible relapsing fever. One day I would have the symptoms very badly, the next day it would be gone, only to return with full force again a few days later. One of the missionaries took it upon herself to nurse me back to health and it was during that time that I began to understand a lot more about the love and care that God has for all people on the earth, no matter what race or culture they come from.

I finally left school and started to train as a teacher. Then someone suggested that I might like to consider becoming an accountant. It seemed a good thing to do and I trained hard and eventually became sought after by big companies looking for honest workers who would not cheat them. I met a wonderful young lady. We married and had several children. All the family attended church each Sunday and our life was pleasant, but in many respects unremarkable.

Many years went by and I was now a man in my mid fifties, and I suppose I thought I had heard and seen most things. Then one Sunday morning our pastor announced that we had some guest speakers from America who would be taking the service. This was quite exciting as we didn't have many foreign visitors to our church. But that morning I was stirred by the message that these visitors brought and when they invited people to go to the front of the church to be prayed for, I was one of the first to my feet. As they prayed for me, I felt such a powerful yet gentle move of God's Holy Spirit go through my body and I knew that I had been truly touched by God. It was then I received a strong urge to preach the Gospel and to tell others about the love of God by whatever means were possible. Even today, many years later, it remains such a strong compulsion within me and I know that it is also a commandment that God has given that He wants to see fulfilled, so that all those that He has called can enter into the Kingdom of God.

After that event a few more years rolled by and eventually the time came when one of my daughters needed to consider her next move as far as her education was concerned. The possibility of her finishing off her education abroad presented itself as a real option and so, within a short space of time, we were packing our bags and heading for England.

We soon settled into our new life in Birmingham. My daughter was happy at her College, my wife and I quickly made friends in the church we started to attend, and I began to look round for opportunities of sharing the Gospel message in this land that had originally brought the Christian faith to Africa. Although I used to preach on a fairly regular basis back home, preaching opportunities didn't come as thick and fast here in Britain. Of course, I knew that wasn't the only way to spread the Gospel and I began to think of other things that I could do to tell people how much God loved them.

I hit on the idea of buying some leaflets which explained briefly and clearly the Christian message that I could give out to people on the street. I bought ones that had Bible verses contained in the text so that anyone could look up the verse for themselves. The leaflet also had an address which anyone could write to if they wanted more information.

I then realised that when I approached people in the street, offering them something to read, they wouldn't know what it was about and might even think it was something political or I was trying to sell something and reject it, therefore possibly rejecting knowing more about God's love. I decided therefore to make a placard which I could wear around my neck with a simple message of God's love on it, so that people taking a leaflet from me would know what my message was all about. Soon I had made a wooden sign which read:

JESUS CHRIST IS LORD!
REPENT THEREFORE AND BE CONVERTED,
THAT YOUR SINS MIGHT BE BLOTTED OUT.

I put a piece of tape on it so that I could wear it around my neck, allowing both of my hands to be free to give out the leaflets. On several occasions I used it without complaint or problems from anyone. It therefore came as a great surprise when I was getting off a train at a busy midlands train station one day, that I was approached by two burly policemen.

"You can't wear that here," said one of them. "You're causing an offence. You'll have to take it off," he said, nodding towards my placard. I looked at him in disbelief. I couldn't believe that this was being said by a policeman in Britain, of all places, where the Gospel message has been taken to all parts of the world for hundreds of years.

"What offence am I committing?" I asked.

Getting out their little black book, the officers said I was committing an offence under the Public Order Act 1986. That didn't mean anything to me of course, but checking up on it later I discovered that the Act said that carrying a placard displaying words which were threatening, insulting or abusive was illegal – but I could hardly think that any of the words on my placard could ever be described as that. I then asked them if anyone had actually made a complaint against me and they said yes, but were unable to produce anyone! I then said that if that was the case, they had better remove the placard from around my neck. They said they were not prepared to do that, which started to get the whole thing into the area of farce. They then said that although I couldn't wear it around my neck, I was able to carry it. That was fine by me – it still contained the same message of Good News! I then went on my way and spent the afternoon giving out my leaflets and chatting to people about the Lord. Returning to the station later that day to make my way home, the over zealous guardians of the law were nowhere to be seen and I made my way home unmolested.

That was, however, not the only time I have discovered that little by little the freedom to talk about Christianity in Britain is steadily being eroded. There are several festivals held up and down the country each year and I and a friend of mine for a good few years have gone along, duly registered our stall, displayed Christian books and leaflets, and from time to time during the day read out portions of scripture such as, *"For God so loved the world that he gave his one and only Son, that whoever believes in him shall not perish but have eternal life"* (John 3:16). But on the last occasion when we began to set up our stall we began to get objections from the organisers, even though we had applied and paid our fee in the normal way. We have never tried to confront people who did not want to hear our message and have always been well received by those attending the festivals. But now we sense that the mood is changing and organisers of functions seem reluctant to have an expression of Christian witness, even though a Muslim stall was in evidence at the same festival.

I am sad at the way things seem to be going in this wonderful country that has in years gone by sent so many missionaries overseas to tell the good news of Jesus to my people and people all around the world. There was a time when I was living a pleasant life in Africa, going to church each Sunday, but making very little impact upon the rest of my community. Then I was touched by the fire of the Holy Spirit and I woke up to the challenge of the Gospel. My prayer is that many Christians in Britain today will wake up to what is happening in their own country at this time and ask that God anoints them with the power of the Holy Spirit to proclaim the Gospel message while they are still able.

In the Spotlight

Becoming a teenager can be difficult in the best regulated households. The years between twelve and twenty are times of great change, physically and emotionally, but most of us survive the ordeal with help from family and friends. But Shirlee had problems that most of us could never even begin to relate to. She was never allowed to have a social life outside of school and by the time she was fifteen things had got so bad that she became a prisoner in her own home. When Shirlee was locked up and beaten by her father she thought things couldn't get much worse – until she discovered that her family were planning to return to Pakistan so that she could marry a man she had never even met...

To be honest, I didn't have the greatest childhood. I was born in Pakistan where my father came from and where my English mother had lived for several years. They had a strange kind of marriage with Dad a lot older than my Mum. The fact that he knew very little English made things even worse as far as communication between them both was concerned. Because of his lack of education he went from one low paid job to the next, never staying in any one for long and often being out of work for lengthy periods. By the time I was seven we were

very poor indeed. It was then that my parents decided to
come to England and stay with my Nan. Of course, I and my
two brothers, who were both younger than I was, had no say
in the matter.

Naturally Mum found it easier than the rest of us to adjust
to life in England, with Dad struggling the most. He had been
brought up under strict Muslim law in a very rural village in
Pakistan where life had changed little over hundreds of years.
Coming to England even electricity was a novelty for him and
he would often amuse himself by flicking the light switches on
and off, trying to discover how the magic worked.

Even though Dad soon picked up unskilled work in his
adopted country, the tensions between him and Mum did not
improve. There were a lot of rows and a lot of violent
behaviour. For him, the only life he knew was living out the
strict rules of Islam and he expected us all to do the same. In
his mind no other faith was valid or should be tolerated. He
was a very difficult man to please and incredibly moody.
When he became moody he also became violent and we all
learned to avoid him as much as we could.

After a while we moved out of my Nan's house as Dad got
work in a different part of the country from where she was
living. I started to attend the local state school, but as soon as I
came home I had to catch up on the prayers that, according to
the Muslim faith, I should have said throughout the day.

Even though I was attending a normal English state school I
was kept at home every Friday, the Muslim holy day. I'm still
not sure how my parents were allowed to get away with this,
but they did, in spite of the fact that they were breaking British
law. So each Friday I, along with my brothers and my sister
who had been born after our arrival in England, were made
to recite the appropriate prayers and observe all the Islamic
rituals.

My first brush with Christianity was around this time. An
elderly couple lived across the road from our house and, as I

was to discover, were both committed Christians. I now realise that they must have been praying for us all as a family and they undoubtedly saw me going to school and coming home each day. They obviously knew enough about Islam to realise that it would not be appropriate to talk to me directly about Jesus. How they got round this was ingenious. They hid several books with a Christian theme under a bush in our front garden and then quickly told me what they had done as I walked past their house one sunny afternoon.

I waited until my Dad was out before smuggling their gift into the house and secretly started to read the books. One book was about children who'd had an encounter with God and one story actually told how a girl became a Christian by asking Jesus to come and take control of her life. I thought that particular chapter was wonderful, but dismissed it as a kind of fairy tale. I couldn't believe that it could be so simple to have an eternal relationship with God. I had no idea that it could actually be true and that this was the personal experience of millions of people living on planet Earth.

Then about a year later a friend of mine at school told me when we were chatting one day that she was a born-again Christian and that she was looking forward to going to heaven when she died. I stared at her open-mouthed, not knowing how to respond. I didn't have the courage to say so to her face, but I reckoned that she must be some kind of nutcase! And how arrogant that she believed that one day she would end up in heaven I thought to myself. When I got home I told my Mum what she had said.

Mum agreed with me. She also believed that no one could ever assume or presume that they would one day be in heaven. "How dare those Christians think that *they* will one day go to heaven," she said angrily. Even with all the prayers and rituals that we went through as practising Muslims, we certainly never had that kind of assurance. Although Mum had been born in Britain she had well and truly adopted the

Muslim faith and was totally immersed in its teachings. Islam was the one thing that united my parents.

In the culture that my Dad came from girls were married off at a very young age and here I was growing up fast with no sign of any wedding on the horizon. But as far as I was concerned, getting married was the last thing on my mind. I was barely into my teens, and not ready for such a huge step mentally, emotionally or physically. British culture said that at thirteen I was just a kid. Thirteen in the culture Dad was from said that I was ready for marriage. But all I wanted to do was to live the kind of life that my friends at school lived. I felt so at home in the English culture and resented the restrictions that my parents and the Muslim faith put upon me. What was so wrong about not wearing a headscarf all the time, or occasionally wanting to wear a pretty dress I thought to myself? I was never allowed to discuss or question anything that I was told to do and now that I was in my teenage years, the normal teenage rebellion started to kick in, which didn't exactly help the already explosive tensions within the family home.

When I got to the ripe old age of fifteen and was still not married this fact started to weigh heavily on my Dad's mind. He began to make plans to take me back to Pakistan to get married to someone that my parents had heard about who sounded eligible to them, but who I had never met. Although plans for our return started to gather momentum fairly quickly, almost up until the point when it was time to go I was not aware of any of this. I was just trying to enjoy my life as much as I could and join in with as many normal activities within the school as the restrictions that my parents put upon me allowed.

One such activity was the annual school production. Rehearsals took place in school time, but then during a few evenings at the end of term parents were invited to see what their children had been working on together. I knew that there was absolutely no chance that my parents would ever attend such an event, but I was concerned as to how I was going to get their permission to be involved. I knew that I had to be very careful about what I volunteered for, especially as this year the production had a distinctly biblical flavour to it, being *Joseph's Amazing Technicolor Dreamcoat*. Everyone in my year was expected to take part in some way or other. I knew that my parents would never agree to me singing and dancing on stage, so I volunteered to work on one of the backstage tasks needed to put the show together. Someone suggested that I might like to help those involved in the lighting of the stage, which I quickly agreed to, hoping that come the big night, my parents would give their permission for me to attend. The problem was that I was never allowed out of the house after I got home from school, not even to go and visit a friend, so I knew that the chances of my being allowed to go out for several consecutive nights to take part in a school production were pretty slim – but embarrassment stopped me sharing any of this with my teacher.

The first night of the production was drawing ever nearer and I still had not found enough courage to tell my parents what we all had been rehearsing for, never mind asking their permission to be involved in the evening performances. The day of the first performance dawned and there wasn't a suitable moment to say anything before I left for school. And after I had said all the prayers and done the study that was expected of me when I got home, it was tea time, and so I hoped for a suitable moment over the meal to broach the subject, which did not come. I looked anxiously at the clock. I needed to be back at school in less than an hour and I still hadn't mentioned anything to my parents.

Driven now by sheer necessity, I blurted out to them what was happening at school and why I needed to go back there within the next hour. They flatly refused to allow me to leave the house. I felt very resentful and panicky all at the same time. I had not told my teacher that I might have a problem in coming back to school in the evening and therefore I knew I would have a lot of explaining to do if I did not turn up as everyone expected me to.

I suddenly heard myself saying to my Mum, "I'm sorry, but I'm going to go anyway." Her instant reply was, "Well, if you go, don't expect to come back again."

With that I picked up my satchel and walked out of the house and made my way towards school, not sure what I would do at the end of the evening. Once I arrived I just tried to concentrate on what I had been trained to do during the show. I found that working the spotlights was quite demanding.

As the show progressed so the tension within me built up too. My Dad was violent to us all as a family and I knew that I would get the full force of his wrath once I returned home. I couldn't work out what my next move should be. By the time the show finished I was very worried about going back home on my own and told my friend Sally – the girl who I had dismissed as a nutcase a couple of years before when she told me that she was a Christian and was looking forward to going to heaven. She went and sought out the Head Teacher. I explained to her the dilemma I was in, while she listened carefully without commenting. She obviously took what I was telling her seriously. Maybe she knew more about my family than I realised. She thought for a moment and then told me to go and sleep at Sally's house that night, saying that she would talk to me again the next day.

Although I did not know it, my parents went onto the streets looking for me that night, without success. The next day they turned up at school and started a huge row which resulted in the Social Services having to be called in. In many ways I felt sorry for Mum and Dad and I could understand why they were so angry – they were worried about me. I knew I had handled the whole thing badly. I should have given them more warning about needing to go back to school.

My parents were furious that I had not come home the previous night, but I knew that if I had returned, I would have been severely beaten. But it seemed that good came from my actions. Somehow or other the Social Services persuaded my parents to let me go and live with my Nan for a while, allowing the tension at home to die down. Amazingly they agreed and within a couple of days they were putting me and a packed suitcase on a train which would take me directly to the town where Nan lived. I felt the pressure lift from me the further I travelled away from home. After a couple of hours the train pulled into the station where my Nan was waiting for me. I didn't have to explain anything to her. She knew my father's violent ways and was glad to have me living with her for a while. She even enrolled me in a local school so that my education would not be interrupted.

After a few days had passed my Mum started to ring my Nan several times a week, saying that Dad was now OK, he had calmed down and was no longer acting violently, and therefore they wanted me to return home. Nan didn't tell me about the calls, but managed to say enough to Mum to allow me to stay living with her. But in the end Nan ran out of excuses why I should continue to stay with her, but she knew that I would be very reluctant to leave the peace and safety of her house, whatever my Mum or Dad were saying. So when the half-term came around, she said she had arranged for me to go and visit a friend who lived in the same town as my parents. I thought this was a great idea and never suspected that what she had actually done was to secretly arrange for my parents and not my friend to be waiting for me at the station.

I should have taken more note of the troubled look on her face when she said goodbye to me and the way that she kept emphasising that she had bought me a *return* ticket and that I must keep it safe and to use it if necessary. I'm sure that if Nan had known what was going to happen to me when I did meet

up with my parents again, she would have never allowed me
to go.

The two hour train journey passed without incident and I
had no idea what I was walking into once the train pulled into
my local station. I managed to clamber out of the train with
my heavy suitcase without too much hassle. And as soon as I
walked off the platform I was scanning the scene for my friend
who I thought would be waiting for me. I started to feel
disappointed when there was no sign of her anywhere.
However, no sooner had I walked through the ticket barrier
than I was grabbed from either side by two people. It all
happened so quickly I hardly had time to react. I then realised
that it was my Mum and Dad, who lifted me off my feet and
began to frogmarch me out of the station. I could see the exit
doors leading out onto the road and my Uncle, also a devout
Muslim, standing there, waiting to get me into his car. I
understood at last what was happening and I started to call out
in a loud voice the name of my friend, who I still thought was
around somewhere waiting for me. As soon as I began to call
out I received a massive blow on my head from my Dad. My
screams and his violence towards me started to attract
attention from those in the immediate vicinity and a couple
of people began to make a note of the registration number of
the car that I was now being pushed into, with Mum trying to
ward them off as best she could. The car took off at high speed
before anyone could do anything and I sat at the back of the
car in a complete daze, still finding it hard to believe that I had
been totally tricked into coming back to live once again with
my parents and all the problems that entailed.

I had gone to live with my Nan in July when the weather
was warm and sunny. Now it was November and as I looked
out of the car window all I could see was cold, grey streets. I
wondered what lay in store for me. An icy silence filled the car
as it rushed down shabby and mainly deserted streets, back to
the family home and whatever awaited me.

It's not pleasant to recall what happened once I returned home. My Dad showed me in his own unique way how displeased he was with me for being away from home for so long. When my punishment was over my day clothes were taken from me and I was given pyjamas to wear and locked in my room. They were going to make absolutely certain sure that I would not leave the house on my own again.

I felt desperate. The thought of being locked up in a small room horrified me. I had no head for heights, but I started to wonder about the chances of getting out of my bedroom window and making my escape that way. I looked out of the window and saw my parents standing in the garden looking up at me – they had already thought about what I might consider and were waiting for any move I might make in that direction. A few minutes later one of my brothers came into my room and the door was locked behind him. He was not there to keep me company, but to make sure that I didn't try to escape. After a couple of hours he was let out and my other brother was let in. I was never allowed to be on my own. Every so often the person that had been detailed to sit with me was told to get out and my Dad would enter the room. After knocking me around a bit and sometimes pulling me around the room with my hair he would try and get me to recite passages from the Qur'an which referred to showing respect to one's parents and then he would attempt to get me to pray to Allah, wanting me to ask forgiveness for the way I had behaved. But I was having none of it. I felt sure that many from the Muslim faith would be outraged if they knew how I was being treated. I was totally miserable and found it impossible to recite the prayers. But I feared that one of Dad's punishment sessions might get totally out of hand if I kept refusing to do what he wanted me to do. I knew I had to escape – but how?

For some reason my mind started to go back to the books that I had been given a few years earlier by the Christian couple who lived over the road. I remembered the true stories of children who were in difficult circumstances and when they prayed to Jesus He came to their rescue. Of course as a Muslim I had always been taught to pray, but those were formal, set prayers. Since reading those books, I had begun to pray to Jesus, just small one sentence prayers now and then, and they always seemed to be answered. I started to think about some of the conversations that I'd had with Sally my friend from school who had become a Christian. She spoke about Jesus as though He was as close to her as any of her other friends. I decided to pray in earnest to Him about my current situation.

"Jesus," I silently prayed, "if You are real, please get me out of this mess before it's too late." That seemed to sum up what I was feeling and I left it at that.

I didn't know it then, but my prayers couldn't have been more timely. My family had already taken the decision to sell up and move back to Pakistan and to take me with them. A wedding was in the process of being arranged for me on our return, as is the custom in certain Muslim circles. The proposed bridegroom was someone I had never met, but someone whose parents my parents had come to some sort of an arrangement with.

Already our furniture had been put up for sale, which accounted for the people who kept coming to the door and then a little later on, taking things away. One day I overheard one of my brothers say to someone that he was talking to on the phone that we would be leaving in about two week's time. Two weeks. I didn't have long to get out of this tight spot I was in. Would Jesus come to my aid? And if He did, how would He do so? I had no idea, but my trust in Him began to grow.

A few days later my Dad came in for one of his "sessions". As he raised his fist to beat me I shouted out in a loud voice, "In the name of Jesus, get behind me Satan." I had no idea what made me say that and I shocked and surprised myself. The reaction that my outburst had on my Dad was even more stunning. He stopped in his tracks, looked very startled and then turned and ran down the stairs shouting to my Mum, "She's calling me Satan!" Dad's English was still not good, but he had picked up on that one word well enough. I noted that he didn't come back that day to continue his session with me.

I knew time was running out and I had to find a way to leave the house without being detected. I thought about tying some of my bedclothes together to make a rope, then tying it to the bath taps and escaping through the bathroom window. Then I remembered that below the bathroom was the kitchen window and I would be seen by anyone who happened to be in there, a room that was occupied by at least one member of the family most of the time, even if I ever got the chance to get the bedclothes to the bathroom. So that was another plan that came to nothing. But I knew I had to do something. It was already a week since I had heard my brother say that they were leaving in about two weeks time.

It had been one of those dull, dreary November days which had turned foggy as night fell. The day was Saturday, so everyone was at home. My youngest brother and my sister were locked in my room with me. We were eating our evening meal together. Suddenly the doorbell rang. My brother said that it was probably the people who had come wanting to purchase the fridge-freezer. My Dad ran down the stairs, shouting to the people at the door to go round the back. We never used the front door which was kept padlocked. A few moments later he called my brother down to give him a hand. Someone came to let him out. They then dashed down the stairs so as not to keep Dad waiting, without locking the door behind them. That left me in my bedroom, which was at the back of the house, with my little sister. I then had to leave the room to wash my hands and as soon as I was on the landing an idea of how I could escape suddenly popped

into my mind. I went into the bathroom, washed my hands
and then left the tap running. I came out of the bathroom and
spotted my sister's trainers on the landing and quickly slipped
them on. The only other things I was wearing were my
pyjamas and dressing gown. I could hear my other two
brothers talking in the other back bedroom and I knew the
rest of the family were downstairs, attending to the people
who were looking at the fridge-freezer in the kitchen. This
meant that for several moments at least, everyone was in the
back of the house. I swiftly walked to the front bedroom,
climbed out of the window onto a ledge above the front door,
even managing to close the window behind me. The houses in
our street were so constructed that the front doors of the
semi-detached houses were side by side, with one continuous
ledge covering both front doors. So I jumped down from
the ledge into next door's garden, walked out of their front
gate and then into the dark November night. I felt very scared
and had no idea where I could go to be safe.

The problem was that my mother was well known in the
area because she worked in the corner shop and as a result of
that most people living nearby knew me also, and would have
immediately taken me back home if I had gone knocking on
their door. But I had to find a safe place to go to quite quickly.
I could not stay outside for long in the low November
temperatures. I had removed my dressing gown as soon as I
had got down from the ledge so as not to appear too
conspicuous to anyone who saw me in the street and the
raw November weather started to bite into me. I needed to
find a place of safety and quickly.

As I started to move swiftly past houses all looking much
the same, half-shrouded as they were in the November
gloom, one house suddenly seemed to stand out from the
rest, for no apparent reason. At that same moment I heard a
voice deep inside me saying, "Go to *that* house." Immediately
I started to walk down the garden path. There was no

hesitation on my part, wondering if I had heard correctly or not – I just instantly did what the voice inside told me to do. I rang the bell and waited for someone to answer. Within a moment the hall light was switched on and I saw the shadow of a man opening the door.

To my relief it was a stranger's face that greeted me and not someone who I recognised. I had chosen, or should I say been directed to, a house where I was not known. I asked if I could come in, giving no reason why. Without hesitation I was taken into their living room. The man and his wife were obviously curious about where I had come from. They hardly knew anyone in the area as they had only moved to this house a couple of weeks before I went to live with my Nan. I can't imagine what they must have thought about me. There I was, on a cold November night, dressed only in pyjamas and trainers, with fairly heavy bruising on my face and around my neck.

A girl about my age came into the room. She went to my school and I recognised her immediately, although she did not recognise me in the state I was in. Then her Mum and Dad, after quickly consulting with each other, agreed that I could stay the night with them and that they would not report my whereabouts to the Police that night. They realised that I just needed a little space from the circumstances that I had been through. I was very grateful to them for that.

The next day dawned and I had breakfast with the family, but then around lunchtime they said they had no alternative but to take me to the Police Station. I understood the difficult situation I had put them into, but I was terrified as I got into their car, knowing what I was in for once I was alone again with my father.

When I arrived at the Police Station, I was very surprised to discover that the Police officer instantly knew who I was. I was even more surprised when he bent down behind the desk, pulled up my suitcase and said, "I believe that this belongs to you." He then told me that it had been given to him by my family who had flown out to Pakistan at 6.30 a.m. that morning!

He proceeded to tell me what had happened since I secretly left the house the evening before. He said that when my parents discovered I was no longer in the house they contacted the Police and then they rang my Head Teacher. When that didn't produce any results my mother found an old address book of mine and systematically rang every number in the book, trying to find out where I was. The reason they wanted to find me so quickly was that they knew they were flying out to Pakistan just hours after I had made my bid for freedom, although I had no idea of their imminent travel plans. I presumed, working on what I had overheard my brother say, that I had at least another week to try and escape. But as it happened, I had managed to run away at the very last possible moment. The house that I had been directed to was not in my address book; the girl who lived there was not in any of my classes and had no association with me, in or out of school. She was just someone I had seen once or twice in the playground before I went to live with my Nan. There was nothing to link me with her, which made that particular house the ideal one to spend the night in. The hiding place that Jesus had prepared for me was perfect and His timing incredibly precise. It was an amazing answer to prayer.

I was put into care for a couple of years and then, by the time I was old enough to go to university, I was able to make my own way in the world. I knew I had to make more enquiries about this man called Jesus who had rescued me when I was in such need. Through the help of several Christian counsellors I asked Jesus into my heart and soon after that forgave my parents totally for the things that had gone on in the past.

I learnt sometime later that my father had died in Pakistan and that my mother had returned to this country with my brothers and sister. She is still a devout Muslim, but one of my brothers and my sister are now Christians, although they came to faith independently of any influence from me.

I hold no malice or ill will towards my parents and what they did to me. Because I know that Jesus has forgiven all my sins I have no option but to forgive all those who have treated me badly, intentionally or unintentionally.

I know that Jesus is a loving Saviour, who answers the prayers of those who put their trust in Him. What happened to me in my childhood and teenage years was not right in any respect, but God used it to show how His tremendous love wants to touch all of mankind.

God arranged for me to be rescued – twice. The first was from the house of punishment and terror, the second was from the clutches of sin. The first was when I left the house in pyjamas and trainers; the second was when I left the kingdom of darkness and entered the kingdom of light. The first was for a few crucial hours, the second was for eternity.

I've been a Christian for quite a few years now and life is still challenging, but in different ways than it was when I was living with my parents. The big difference is that I now have a loving Heavenly Father that I can take my problems to, and just like my friend Sally, I know that when I die I will be with Him forever. Jesus said, *"If the Son sets you free, you will be free indeed"* (John 8:36). Sometimes I feel like He spoke those words just for me!

Michael's Real-Life Drama

There was always something that had drawn Michael to the world of theatre and as a kid he dreamed of getting involved in that glamorous environment. So when he was sixteen he decided to make preparations towards what he hoped would be his future career by getting on a drama course. But he found himself in the midst of a real life drama where he was centre stage as he struggled to defend his faith against his tutors and fellow students who seemed to delight in confronting his beliefs whilst defending all that was blasphemous and lewd. This is his story.

For some people the claims of Christianity are something that they are not exposed to until they go to school or college, if at all. But because my parents are Christians I learnt from an early age the stories of the Bible and they explained to me that even though Jesus had died on the Cross to deal with the sins of the world, I had to personally accept what He had done for me and then invite Jesus to come and live in my heart. Although I was only seven at the time my encounter with God was real. But it wasn't until my teenage years that I really started to take my faith seriously. I enjoyed attending the local Baptist church where several of my friends also went.

Around that time I had to decide what I wanted to do with my life and because I had always had an interest in the theatre I decided to apply for a place on the drama course at the local technical college. To my delight I was accepted and at first things seemed to be going fine. But after just a few short weeks I began to get an uneasy feeling about what I had signed up for. I started to realise that there were aspects of the course that clashed with my basic beliefs and standards. Not only was everyone on the course asked to study and attend plays and films portraying deviant lifestyles and foul language, but we were also told to act out these lifestyles as part of our studies. I'm no wet blanket, but some of the stuff that we were now starting to concentrate on could only be described as blasphemous or bordering on the pornographic – but it was all done in the name of "free expression".

If this wasn't bad enough, the tutors soon cottoned on to the fact that I was a Bible-believing Christian, so as word got round, I and another Christian on the course started to be targeted. Lectures would be opened up on debates such as whether or not Jesus was a homosexual or whether He'd ever had sex with Mary Magdalene. The teachers seemed eager to drag me into the debate so that I was forced to defend my views against those held by the lecturers and the rest of the class. I often felt intimidated, especially as the tutors were so much older than I was. It then became obvious that the other Christian on my course, a girl called Lucy, seemed more and more reluctant to express an opinion during these debates. She seemed to prefer to keep in the background, even though I knew she was a believer.

I understood all too well how difficult it was to defend what I knew to be right, so I presumed that she was struggling just as much with these issues as I was. I decided to talk to her about things one day, to get her thoughts on what was going on. I managed to catch her just as she was leaving the college.

When I asked if we could talk for a few moments, she seemed edgy and nervous, looking around all the time, as if she didn't really want to be seen talking to me. Not wanting to put it off any longer I began to tell her how I was finding the course difficult because of the way that Christianity was always been ridiculed and wondered what her thoughts on everything were.

She told me that she thought that I was taking my Christianity too seriously and that I shouldn't be bothered about what we were all asked to say and do, but just conform, like everyone else on the course.

With that, Lucy made her excuses and left, making me feel even more vulnerable than I felt before talking to her. The one person I thought I might have got some backing from was obviously nailing her colours firmly to the fence! I thought through carefully what she had said, of course, but ended up feeling that doing what Lucy suggested sounded too much like selling out to all my principles that I believed Jesus wanted me to stick to. I then thought it might be good to chat things over with some of my Christian friends at church. I guessed they would understand the dilemma I was in and maybe have some advice for me that I could put into practice. But as I started to talk to them I began to realise that they would not give me any more support or sympathy than I got from Lucy. They either didn't understand or didn't want to understand the situation I found myself in.

One guy, called Neil, who was a keen Christian before he started to date his non-Christian girlfriend, said that he thought people could take Christianity too far, that life was how it was and we had to just go along with what society dished out. He said I ought to lighten up a little and that as long as I got through the course what did it matter? The others didn't say much but looked on impatiently, more interested in their half-finished game of pool than debating how to stand up for the faith that they all said they believed in.

I knew, however, that it wasn't just a case of lightening up, but *standing up* for the standards and beliefs that I had known since I was a child. The more I thought and prayed about what others had said, the more convinced I was that God didn't want me to compromise my faith, no matter how much I wanted a career in the theatre.

Although I had shared my problems and concerns first of all with Lucy and then the guys at church, I hadn't wanted to bother my parents, so they had no idea of the dilemma I was in. But after a while they began to notice something was wrong as I started to let the problems that I was having at college travel home with me. After I had told them what had been going on, they offered me their support and some good advice. Mum suggested that I have a word with Jim Carmichael, our Pastor, saying that he might have come across a similar kind of situation before and would therefore know what to do. I reckoned paying him a visit was worth a shot and so a few days later I was sat in his study, telling him everything that had gone on as clearly and accurately as I could. He was great, listening carefully to all that I had to tell him, only interrupting to clarify a point here or there. At the end of what I had to tell him, he sat back in his chair with a thoughtful look on his face.

"Well, I certainly appreciate you telling me all of this – and the way you have handled it," he told me. "More and more in our society we see Christian principles and standards ignored or ridiculed and from my own experience it seems to be getting worse rather than better." He stopped, obviously thinking how best he could help. It reminded me of how he would sometimes pause during a sermon before making an important point. Then he started to speak again.

"How would you feel if I went to have a word with your tutor? I'm probably being a little naïve in saying this, but it just might be that he doesn't fully understand why you are taking the stance that you are and once he is put in the picture, the whole thing might change. Hopefully it could all get sorted once I've been to see him."

I agreed, happy that something seemed to be happening at last, but pessimistic about how my tutor would react. As it turned out, I had every reason to be.

Jim drove over to the college in order to see the tutor and quickly tried to explain as simply as he could why he was there and how I was feeling. But instead of the two men having a normal conversation together, Mr Carmichael soon found himself on the receiving end of a load of verbal abuse from my tutor who totally defended every foul word, every lewd act, every obscenity that he had subjected the course to read, say or act, as well as the discussions about Christianity that he had roped me into.

After that, there seemed only one way to go as far as I was concerned. With a heavy heart I resigned from the course and turned my attention to other things. I was prepared to work hard and get good grades on the course I had enrolled for – but not at any price. My Christian faith meant more to me than what I was being asked to say and do on a regular basis.

That could have been where this sad and sordid tale ended, but I was determined not to be blown off course by the things I experienced. I'm now at university doing media studies and although I continue to come across similar attitudes and stances to those I experienced on my drama course, I am now better equipped to deal with them and am able to avoid the things that are not right to get involved in as a Christian.

I'd advise any Christian, young or old, never to compromise their faith and standards. Christians are meant to be a light in a world of darkness, but how can we be that if we are not standing up for all the darkness and depravity that is around us? Although I regret what I had to go through, I don't hold any resentment to those who made me go through it. Because I turned the whole thing over to God it ended up being a valuable experience and it has actually strengthened my own personal walk with Him. During the darkest days I would look forward eagerly to each Sunday, when I could have fellowship with other believers and hear the Word of God faithfully preached. And if for whatever reason I didn't make it to church on a Sunday, I found it doubly hard to face everything that was going on at the drama course on the Monday morning. Christians are strongest when we stand together and support each other. As Christians we need to know what we believe and be prepared to stand up for those beliefs. I know that I'm glad that I did.

Playing with Fire

Brought up on the hard streets of Glasgow there wasn't too much love in Julie's life – until she was invited on holiday by a school friend to a Christian camp, where she heard the Good News of Jesus and discovered how to become a Christian. But with no one to encourage her in her new found faith she had to wait until becoming an adult before her faith was re-ignited and she joined a church. Julie thought she knew better than her Christian friends when they warned her not to get too friendly with the handsome Muslim who wanted to marry her. Ignoring their advice, her dream marriage slowly turned into a nightmare as she was insulted, physically attacked and abused by her husband before the Courts decided that her children should be taken from her...

I was born and brought up in Glasgow. Playing on city streets with the occasional visit to the local park was as good as it got for me, until I was around the age of ten. Then one day a school friend of mine told me that she was going on holiday to some sort of camp in the country with a load of other children and wondered if I would be allowed to go along too. To my surprise my Mum said I could go – the fact that it was a children's camp organised by the local church probably made her feel that it would be a good safe holiday for me, even though as a family we never had contact with any church. I had a brilliant time away from home, but the greatest impact for me was hearing about Jesus and how much He loved me. *No one* had ever told me that before. I was also told that I could ask Him to come into my heart, which meant that He would then be with me forever. I took that very important step and not only did Jesus make His home in my heart, but I was filled with His Holy Spirit too. I was so excited and told one of the adults who were in charge of running the camp what I had done. Looking back I now realise that I obviously chose the wrong person to tell. She just said, "Oh, that's nice dear," in a very condescending way and I remember feeling so disappointed that she hadn't shown more interest. Before I had a chance to tell others my news it was time to go back home and with no one to encourage me in my Christian life I quickly lost all the joy I had felt and didn't develop at all as a Christian, even though the experience I'd had was genuine.

I had to wait another twenty years before my love for the Lord began to grow again and I started to look for a church that I could belong to. I began to realise that being a Christian was not as easy as I had thought. In the process of trying to have fellowship with other Christians I had got involved with what I now know was a cult – a group of people who appeared to be Christians, but when you scratched the surface it became clear that some of the beliefs that they held were not biblically correct. I was with them for eight weeks before I had the good sense to part company with them, but I now realise that my involvement with that group of people undermined my confidence and ability to make good decisions.

But something else was also happening to me at this time that was to make an even greater impact on my life and in many ways would be a greater threat to my Christian life. It all started in the most beguiling way. I was introduced by a friend to a man called Rish. He was a young, handsome Middle Eastern man who quickly swept me off my feet. He was everything that I could dream of in a boyfriend and a potential husband – apart from the fact that he was a Muslim and had no interest in becoming a Christian . . .

After leaving the cult I found a good sound church to attend and when they got to hear of my friendship with Rish their advice to me was brief and to the point: "Don't get too involved with him because he is not a Christian. If you do your own spiritual life will suffer." But I knew better didn't I? To be honest, I actually did try to follow their advice, but every time I told him that I didn't want to see him any more his friends would ring up and tell me that he was almost suicidal and that I should go back with him as he couldn't live without me. I felt under tremendous pressure and in the end I caved in and soon we were making wedding plans. We eventually got married in the local registry office – not the dream wedding I had hoped for, but I really did love Rish and I felt sure that he loved me too.

Things were fine for the first seven years. We had two gorgeous little boys, Rish seemed to be enjoying his work as a bus driver and I loved being a mum. Then one day he announced that he wanted to go back to his own country for a holiday. This surprised me as I knew that he had originally entered the UK as a political refugee. I told him that if he wanted to go, that was fine with me. Then he changed his mind. He now started to say that he wanted to pack up, leave England for good and go and live back in the Middle East. He felt that the situation had changed enough for him to do that. Again I agreed. I remembered what Ruth had said to Naomi about Naomi's people becoming Ruth's people etc. I felt as a loyal wife I should be prepared to follow where my husband wanted me to go. Then he dropped the bombshell.

"We need to get married before we can go and live in Abu Dhabi."

I looked at him in disbelief. "What are you talking about?" I said. "We *are* married."

"Not as far as my country's authorities are concerned," he told me. "They don't recognise marriages carried out in Britain. We need to have an Islamic wedding."

Well, if that's what it takes, that is what I will do, I thought, not knowing that part of the ceremony meant that I would have to convert to Islam, denouncing my faith in Jesus. This was something that the Christian organisation that I was working for at the time quickly made me aware of.

I suddenly remembered a couple of scriptures that the Lord had given me six months earlier which didn't seem to make any kind of sense at the time. They were both from the Gospel of Matthew. The first one said, *"Whoever disowns me before men, I will disown him before my Father in heaven"* (Matthew 10:33) and the second one was, *"Do not be afraid of those who kill the body but cannot kill the soul. Rather, be afraid of the One who can destroy both soul and body in hell"* (Matthew 10:28). When the Lord first gave them to me, I kept saying to Him, "Lord, I just don't know what this is all about. You know I would never deny you." Now I began to understand a little more clearly why the Lord had given me those scriptures.

Now Rish started to put all sorts of pressure on me to convert to Islam. I resisted as hard as I could. Then one day he came home and told me that he'd met a famous British TV personality that day, who also happened to be a Christian. Not only that, but before becoming famous he had been ordained as a Christian minister. Rish had told this guy about our situation and had managed to get his mobile phone number off him. Rish told me to ring him and get some advice. I did ring him up and we chatted for almost an hour, but really the only advice he ended up giving me was to follow my heart and listen to what God was saying to me. My problem was that because of all the pressure that was coming my way I could no longer work out what God was saying to me. But deep down I knew it would be terribly wrong to convert to Islam and I somehow found enough courage to tell Rish that I couldn't go through with what he was asking me to do.

What followed was three days of absolute hell – it's too awful to recall and I have blocked a lot of it from my mind. He would begin to shout and scream at me, his face going purple and contorted. At one point, in a rage, he picked me up and literally threw me out of the house! It was almost as though he was possessed. I was silently praying of course the whole time, but it was only when I started to pray with real authority that his anger stopped as quickly as it had started. It was as though the house was suddenly cleansed. Then Rish turned and said to me, "I know I should feel bitter towards you, but I don't," and then he calmly walked off and made himself a cup of tea!

I went into my bedroom and started to thank God that it was all over, but the Lord said to me, "No, it's not all over. That was just the beginning." When God told me that I felt gutted. How could anything be worse than what I had just been through, I wondered.

In spite of what the Lord had said to me this was the start of a period of calm. I became pregnant again and had a beautiful baby daughter. We moved house and the horrors of the past seemed to be behind us. Then Rish's sister arrived from Abu Dhabi and everything started to crank up again. I heard her on the phone trying to make plans with various Mullahs for an Islamic wedding ceremony to take place between Rish and me, which would also involve me converting to Islam.

"Why can't we just get married in a way that will be recognised by the authorities in Abu Dhabi, but which would not involve me having to convert to Islam?" I asked him one day in desperation.

"Well, yes, that could happen," he said. His eyes seemed to grow cold and distant as he continued to talk to me. I felt hopeful for a moment, until he continued, "However, that would mean that if you just went through the marriage ceremony, but did not convert as well, you would not be recognised as my wife, just my concubine and I would have a ninety-nine year lease on you." That was obviously not the perfect solution as far as I was concerned!

I now had to be on my guard all the time. Because his sister was around I not only had Rish to deal with, but her too. On a couple of occasions they almost succeeded in getting me to a mosque to go through the necessary ceremony, but on both occasions the Lord intervened at the last minute. I knew now, however, that they would not give up until they were successful and when I heard a third attempt being planned I knew I had to make a move – and quickly.

I had my baby daughter with me, but not my two sons. One was in playschool and the other was in day school. I knew that if I didn't act swiftly it would be too late. I had heard his sister making plans to have my daughter taken from me. I decided to leave the house, but I had to do it in such a way that I would not arouse suspicion. We had two cars and Rish said that I should go straight to the mosque in one car with our daughter and he would pick up the boys from school and take them to the mosque. I didn't dare object. Then, just as we were both leaving the house, the phone rang. It was the mosque saying that for some reason or other they had to cancel the ceremony. I had been spared again! But the idea did not go away in Rish's mind or his sister's. I knew my reprieve would not last long.

I was correct in my assumption. A few weeks later they came to me and told me that they had arranged a marriage ceremony for me that did not also involve me having to convert to Islam. Rish was very insistent that I go through with it and by this time I was worn out with all the rows and pressure. What harm could it do, I thought, it's just another marriage ceremony.

So I went to the mosque and the ceremony went ahead. But for the amount I understood of what was going on, it could have been almost anything that I was committing myself to. Although I knew some Arabic by this time, there was no way that I understood even a quarter of what was being said. All I knew was at the end of it all I was handed a marriage certificate. Maybe this will bring some peace into my life again, I thought, but I was soon to learn that the certificate meant that Rish was now legally able to take the children to Abu Dhabi whenever he wanted to! A few days after the ceremony Rish's sister went back home.

Although Rish and I were now legally married in the eyes of the Abu Dhabiian authorities, that still did not satisfy him. He still wanted me to convert to Islam. This was the source of endless rows, when he would shout at me, scare the children and sometimes withhold money which I needed to buy food for us all. His moods started to get blacker and I began to be very afraid of him. I could also see fear in the eyes of our children when he came home from his work. Once again I asked the Lord to guide me. There seemed no one else that I could turn to.

It was around that time that I heard about a refuge centre that was available for women like me. I didn't want to think about having to take the children to such a place, but I was running out of options. Even my pastor seemed to agree that it might be the best course of action. I was very undecided, in spite of what was going on. Then, Rish's sister paid us another visit from Abu Dhabi. She had only been with us a day or two when I heard her talking on the phone, making arrangements to have the children sent to Abu Dhabi. I didn't know what to do. I had to be so careful what I said and did. Rish had now got to the point where he would threaten to divorce me in front of the children, which of course upset them greatly. One day, when he returned from work, he started to shout at me yet again. I thought that if I did not answer back it might calm him down. But the opposite was true. Because I did not respond, he got my clothes and threw them out on the street.

Our little daughter was screaming and crying, really frightened now, and Rish started to shout very loudly saying that I *must* sign the document that would make me a Muslim. I told him, very forcefully, that I could not do that. My daughter was sittting on my knee and I was trying to calm her down. Suddenly Rish snatched the child from me then picked me up and threw me onto the street! There I was surrounded by my clothes, not quite knowing what to do next. I sensed that the neighbours were watching to see what I would do. On previous occasions I had hammered on the door to be let back in. This time I decided on a different tactic. I went round to a friend's house, had a good cry, then together we just prayed to the Lord, telling Him what was going on and asking Him what to do next. Although Rish had never been violent with the children, I did start to wonder what he might do next as he had got himself into such a rage. My friend agreed with me that maybe the best thing I could do was to tell the Police what was going on. I was nervous about getting them involved, but it seemed the wisest thing to do.

I was surprised to discover how helpful and understanding the Police were when I told them what had been happening. They agreed to go with me back to the house and to my astonishment and relief, after speaking briefly to Rish, they quickly rounded up the children and told me that I could take them with me. I had nowhere to go, other than my friend's house. I knew that it would not be safe to stay there for long. Now it seemed that the only safe place left to run to was the refuge centre that I had heard about some time before.

Life at the refuge centre was not great. I didn't feel safe there, even though it was miles from where I had been living with Rish. But every time I prayed about it, the Lord gave me scriptures to reassure me that I and the children were safe. Then after a few months, I did a really silly thing. All the women at the refuge centre seemed to have a lawyer and so I got myself one, and got him to issue a notice to say that Rish could not take the children out of the country – in spite of the fact that the Lord had told me they would be safe. It was through that Court Order that he discovered where we were living and soon I was attending a court hearing that he had arranged, to get custody of the children. I still don't know how it was all allowed to happen, but the Court granted permission not only for him to have access to the children, but to be the one to look after them also! I couldn't believe it. There was nothing that I could do. I went back to the refuge centre, this time on my own. I was in a state of shock and for the next two weeks I hardly got an hour of sleep.

I eventually got a copy of the report that was submitted to the Court, which caused them to let Rish have authority to look after the children. The report was full of lies about me, saying among other things that I was the member of a cult, when actually I was attending the local Assemblies of God church! I was now only allowed to visit my children on a Saturday and then I had to be supervised during the time of my visit. The other stipulation was that I was not allowed to take them near any church or let them have any contact with church members.

I have always been concerned about the plight of perse-cuted Christians and I had literature in the house concerning Christians in certain parts of the Middle East who had suffered persecution. Rish found it and threatened to tell the author-ities in his country what he had read. He even started to come along to the church that I was attending. This was not because he was interested in Christianity, but simply to make trouble. He hated the fact that I was a Christian and that I wanted to stay true to my Christian beliefs rather than become a Muslim like him. It was a very difficult time.

In the end, after going back and forth to the courts, I was allowed to have the children from Friday afternoon until Monday morning. I was also allowed to take them along to a church – as long as it was a "mainstream" church. The authorities must have believed that the Assemblies of God was a cult! I tried going along to various mainstream churches, but some didn't have anything for children and others were just so dead that even I didn't want to be there, never mind the children, who by this time had been told by their dad that Christians were weak and evil and best avoided. At this point they were eight, five and three years old.

The whole situation had taken a terrible toll on them. Their father was still determined to take them to Abu Dhabi and I was involved in over eighteen court cases, all to do with either stopping him from taking them to Abu Dhabi or getting better access to them for myself. Our second son started to comfort eat and he put on a huge amount of weight. Our daughter became very hyperactive and our eldest son became very rude and disrespectful.

There is no happy ending to this story. Well, not at this point anyway. The marital home is up for sale and I don't know what will become of any of us. But I don't blame God for any of this. I was a young Christian who made a lot of foolish mistakes. I knew the scriptures about being "unequally yoked" (2 Corinthians 6:14) but I felt I knew better than God! Marrying someone from the Muslim faith has brought so much pain and sadness into my life and ultimately into the lives of our children. I thought I could play with fire – but now I know that those who do always get their fingers burnt in the end. Maybe someone reading this will be prevented from going through what I have endured.

PART 2

What to Do Next

There are usually at least two things running through my mind whenever I finish a book that I have enjoyed and been challenged by. The first is a feeling of satisfaction that I have managed to read it through to the end with so many other things calling upon my time. The second is a kind of loss, having parted company with characters in the book that I had begun to get emotionally involved with, together with a sense of frustration as I realise that I have no way of helping those whose stories I have read.

I wonder how you felt when you came to the end of the stories in this book? Were you still thinking about how in the story entitled *In the Spotlight* Shirlee was being forced by her family to marry a man she did not know when only fifteen years of age? Or maybe you still feel indignant after reading in *A Storm in a Coffee Cup* how Margaret and her fellow Christians were treated by the authorities when they offered help to someone who nobody else seemed to be doing anything for? Perhaps you are still nursing a sense of frustration and anger after reading how young Michael in *Michael's Real-Life Drama* had to endure so much ridicule from people in authority who ought to have known far better. Each chapter has the potential to stir up strong emotions of one kind or another.

Hopefully, as you have read this book, you have not just been informed but challenged by the whole question of persecution of Christians in a land that many still think of as

a Christian country. If that is the case then this part of the
book has been written for you, so that you can use those
feelings as fuel to do some practical things that could help
change the spiritual climate. You may have presumed that
there is little that one individual can do to change things for
the better. But if so, you would be wrong. There are a number
of actions that most people could take which will certainly
move things on in a positive direction. I have set out below
several steps that can be taken by anyone who wants to see
the right kind of change come about.

1. Do a Spiritual Health Check

The first thing is to check out one's own personal walk with
God. Before we can go out and change the world we need
to be honest with ourselves and ask if anything within our
own lives needs adjusting. This need not (and should not)
be a "heavy" exercise with lots of introspection and self-
condemnation. And we certainly don't need to wait until we
are perfect before we can be used – if that were the case we
would all be waiting forever! But with the help of the Holy
Spirit we should look at our lives as honestly as we can, in an
effort to deal firmly with anything that God shows is a
hindrance in working effectively for Him. Once we've done
that we will then be more able to tackle other forces which are
at large within our society and culture that can make
Christians less than effective in their service to God. If you
are unsure how to proceed, read and consider slowly the
following passage from Philippians and allow the Lord to
speak into your life through the Holy Spirit.

> *"Therefore if you have any encouragement from being united with*
> *Christ, if any comfort from his love, if any common sharing in the*
> *Spirit, if any tenderness and compassion, then make my joy complete*
> *by being like-minded, having the same love, being one in spirit and of*

one mind. Do nothing out of selfish ambition or vain conceit. Rather in humility value others above yourselves, not looking to your own interests but each of you to the interests of the others. In your relationships with one another, have the same attitude of mind Christ Jesus had:

> *Who being in very nature God,*
>   *did not consider equality with God something*
>   *to be used to his own advantage;*
> *rather, he made himself nothing*
>   *by taking the very nature of a servant,*
>   *being made in human likeness.*
> *And being found in appearance as a human being,*
>   *he humbled himself*
>   *by becoming obedient to death – even death on a cross!*
> *Therefore God exalted him to the highest place*
>   *and gave him the name that is above every name,*
> *that at the name of Jesus every knee should bow,*
>   *in heaven and on earth and under the earth,*
> *and every tongue acknowledge that Jesus Christ is Lord,*
>   *to the glory of God the Father.*

Therefore, my dear friends, as you have always obeyed – not only in my presence, but now much more in my absence – continue to work out your salvation with fear and trembling, for it is God who works in you to will and to act in order to fulfil his good purpose. Do everything without grumbling or arguing, so that you may become blameless and pure, 'children of God without fault in a warped and crooked generation.' Then you will shine among them like stars in the sky as you hold firmly to the word of life. And then I will be able to boast on the day of Christ that I did not run or labour in vain. But even if I am being poured out like a drink offering on the sacrifice and service coming from your faith, I am glad and rejoice with all of you. So you too should be glad and rejoice with me."

(Philippians 2:1–18 TNIV)

Often we are not aware of the culture that we live in and the effect that it has upon us until we are in a different environment from our own. That became apparent to me the first time I went to the USA. When I arrived I couldn't understand why I felt so alien in a country that consisted mainly of people who looked like me and talked the same language, but with a different accent! The differences were not obvious at first, but were enough to make me feel unsettled and out of place without really knowing why. Looking back, I now realise that not only were the clothes that people were wearing quite different in style from current fashions in the UK, but so were the cars, the buildings and the food. Even the way people kept telling me to *have a nice day* was not something I would have heard said much in the little Oxfordshire village I was living in at the time. It was only when I reminded myself that I was in a foreign country with a different culture that I started to relax and enjoy the experience.

In a small way I suppose I was experiencing some of the feelings that Muslims, coming new to the Christian faith, experience when they try and integrate into the Christian Church. Often they prefer to continue to wear their traditional clothes and eat the food that they have always been used to, whilst often looking physically different from their new brothers and sisters in the faith whose style of dress and diet, as well as culture, is probably firmly based in the West. The cultural differences at first glance might appear minor, but it still takes determination for the new believer and the church fellowship they have joined not to let differences, big or small, become barriers to total acceptance and integration.

Have you noticed how the culture within the UK in the past few years has changed and is one that is more and more at odds with Christian culture? I'm thinking of things like quiz shows, reality programmes and talent contests that, rather than encouraging people to do well, delight in voting participants off the show with no reward, sneering at their efforts to succeed and enjoying seeing people humiliated. I'm thinking of newspapers that have long discovered that good news doesn't sell newspapers, so revel in the collapse of the marriages of the rich and famous, or appear to be delighted when they discover that someone in the public eye has transgressed in one way or another. I'm thinking of television "soaps" which bear little resemblance to any street or community I know of, where characters habitually shout in each other's faces as a normal way of communicating and extra marital relationships are taken as an everyday occurrence. Add all that to the very real and sadly regular ritual of a significant minority of young people totally overloading themselves with alcohol each weekend and in so doing put their future health in grave danger, not to mention the present welfare of the rest of the population as these teens to thirty-somethings spill out on to the streets in the early hours of the morning, being dreadfully ill, becoming violent with each other and then attacking the authorities when they come to their aid! These actions show all the signs of a lost and empty society in freefall mode, which ultimately impacts upon us all and bears little or no resemblance to the kind of society that Jesus talked of, where love, care and kindness rule.

The laws that God gave to Moses which instructed the Israelites how to live, known as the Ten Commandments, and which once formed the basis of the British legal system, have at best now become the Ten Suggestions. The more society moves away from the standards which God knew would make for a just and stable community, the more everything begins to unravel, with doubt and suspicion spreading like a cancer throughout the land. So at one end of the spectrum husbands and wives are at odds with each other, making divorce an ever increasing option, whilst at the other end giant financial institutions question the integrity of those that they deal with and risk losing their fortunes by trading with the wrong companies at the wrong time.

I had a dream a few years ago and in the dream people were sitting around a camp fire, somewhere in the desert. At the start of the dream the fire was burning brightly, but as the people chatted amongst themselves a breeze blew some sand on the camp fire. The amount of sand was small enough not to concern those in the group and in fact most of them didn't even notice that it had happened, but as the evening progressed more and more sand was blown onto the fire with increasing frequency. And each time it happened a bit more of the fire was extinguished. Then finally the wind blew for the last time and it was strong enough to blow sufficient sand on the embers to put it out completely, leaving the company of people without light or heat and with no means of enjoying once more the warmth and illumination that they had known.

I sometimes wonder if we as Christians are like that camp fire crowd. Do we allow the sands of the culture in which we live to blow over our Christian lives, lessening our impact on an unbelieving world desperate to see true faith in Jesus lived out in the lives of His followers? Do they, instead, see a Church compromised and weakened by the culture that it is surrounded by? As Christians we really must not allow sand of any kind to cover the truth and vitality of the Gospel message. The freedoms we have in this country of ours have been long fought for, but could be quickly lost.

Every motorist will tell you that even the best designed cars have "blind spots" where drivers just cannot see what is happening from where they are sitting in the car. This problem is sometimes overcome by adding extra mirrors, or by drivers asking their passengers to tell them what they can see from *their* vantage point. The truth is that each of us has spiritual blind spots in our own lives, areas that could cause us trouble, and areas that are sometimes apparent to those who are closest too us, but are often too polite to comment upon! An immediate example that springs to mind is the mum I know who loves her children and has made sure that they attend church each Sunday – but can't see any harm in totally engrossing them in books that make the occult appear exciting, without ever pointing out the real mental health dangers and spiritual bondage which almost inevitably come with any brush with the forces of darkness, however innocently packaged they may be. Or the dad who is in full-time Christian work, but allows his kids to get involved in youth activities that seem harmless enough, but have their roots in Eastern religions. Or the church youth worker who can't commit to reading her Bible *every* day, but would never miss the daily reading of her horoscope. What is your blind spot? What is mine? Are you brave enough to ask a friend to tell you if they might know and then in an even braver move, ask the Holy Spirit to get rid of it for you? I wonder if you might prayerfully consider what effect books like *Harry Potter* and *The da Vinci Code* and practices like Yoga, TM and astrology have on our society and those within and without the Christian Church and possibly your own life.

I recently watched a portrayal of Jesus on television. As a believer I found it very difficult viewing. The Jesus that this play portrayed looked unkempt and shifty, a person who needed constant reassurance from those around him, as well as doing and saying things which were entirely from the imagination of the writer and nothing at all to do with the Jesus recorded in the Bible. In other words, the depiction of Jesus was a total travesty of what it should have been, but as I watched I was challenged to ask just what aspect of Jesus do believers and non-believers see when they look at me, one of His followers? Am I even close to being a dim reflection of what He is or is the "sand of the desert" obscuring what others should see? It's a question that we all might ask ourselves.

So, change and movement and progression in our spiritual lives is something that we should all be aiming for. It is then as Christians we can begin to make a better impact on our society. After that the question then is 'What next?'

2. Get into the Community

Have you ever stopped to think just how much of a difference your presence in the community makes, especially if you use your time and energies thoughtfully and prayerfully? Jesus told us not to hide our light under a bushel! But how, you might ask, is that worked out on a practical day to day basis? Well, one way could be to start going where the people are, places like pubs, clubs, evening classes, places where people meet together within the community. You would be amazed how lonely some people can be and to see a friendly face can make all the difference. This type of ministry could have an enormous impact, especially on people with Muslim backgrounds who are struggling with our "semi-detached" society. And the problem spills over into the Christian Church as far as many believers from a Muslim background are concerned.

Let me explain what I mean. In our culture, "fellowship" often means just ten minutes of casual chat over a cup of tea after a Sunday morning service, which has maybe lasted for a hour or a little more. Then the chances of seeing that person again, except maybe at a home group for a couple of hours in the week, are remote. But the Islamic faith is all-embracing and there is generally far more interaction between Muslims on a day to day basis than most Christians ever have. One of the things that Muslims who have become believers have said to me time and again when I chatted with them is how lonely they feel, especially those who, because of their new found faith have been forced to give up their relationships with family members. You could fill the gap by becoming an adopted mum or dad, brother or sister, to a lonely believer new to the faith and maybe new to our culture. Or you could be a friend that supplies their need in some way or another. I guarantee that you will get at least as much out of the relationship as you give to those you have befriended. Let me give you a very small example.

Years ago, when our children were still small, a man came into the Cotswold village in which we were living and took up a very lowly job within the community which paid quite a meagre wage. We discovered that Amir had recently arrived from a Muslim country with his wife. They too had a few children, roughly the same age as ours. As it happened, money was also tight for us at that time and often friends would pass on their still usable clothes for our children to wear. Because our children grew so fast, there was still a lot of wear in the clothes when our kids had finished with them. We hesitated about offering clothes to Amir's family, wondering if they would be offended. We need not have worried. They were as grateful for the free clothes as we were. This simple act was the first link in a chain of friendship that was to grow between us. Then we discovered that Amir and his family had been given a council house close by to where we were living. Now we saw them on a regular basis and our children often played together.

Over the next few years the fortunes of Amir's family improved greatly and he ended up in the catering business. It's a fact that he became much wealthier than us, but it is also true that we could never pass his establishment without being offered a free meal! When we first got to know Amir and his family, it took a bit of courage on our part to begin to relate to someone from a completely different culture, as Amir and his family were one of the first people that we had met from that background and we were not sure whether our friendship would be accepted or not. And from their side, I guess it took just as much courage to begin to relate to a family so different in many ways from theirs. But one thing we both recognised was that under the skin we are all the same, with the same hopes, fears and dreams. I would now confidently say to anyone that we need to stop distrusting Muslims or people from Islamic dominated parts of the world and start loving them, just like God loves them. Don't be put off by their different clothes or the smell of the different kind of food that they eat. That is all so superficial. Basically, people across the globe have the same hopes and fears and many Muslims are so because they have never been given an alternative to consider, and have never heard the good news that Jesus wasn't just a great prophet, but is the promised Messiah who God sent because He loved the whole world so much (John 3:16).

There are two excellent resources that I would recommend. The first is *Distinctly Welcoming – Christian presence in a multifaith society* by Richard Sudworth. Published by Scripture Union (ISBN 978-1-844273-17-1), it is practical guide to the core issues and challenges facing Christians and churches in their engagement with those of other faiths. The other book is *Friendship First* by Steve Bell. There is no better basic guide that will help you understand ordinary Muslims and the culture and ideology from which Muslim background believers have come.

If you are fortunate enough to go on foreign holidays, pray before you go about who you might meet on your journey and possible things you might be able to take along to give to those who are already believers, as well as those who are not. It is amazing how opportunities open up if you are aware of what the Holy Spirit might be doing just because you, as a Christian, are in that part of the world.

Some time ago my wife and I went on holiday to a country that is high on the list of countries where Christianity is forbidden and where there are very few known believers. Whenever we go away on holiday we always take some Christian music along with us, as well as books and teaching tapes. On this particular holiday one man was allocated by the hotel to service our room each day, both morning and evening. He was a good worker who took pride in what he did and we enjoyed passing the time of day with him whenever we saw him.

One evening, about half way through the holiday, we were

late getting out for our evening meal and he came along as usual to tidy our room. The music we had been listening to as we got ready was still playing when he arrived. He stopped what he was doing, listened for a few moments and then said in his broken English, "Beautiful music." I told him that it was a song about how life is sometimes hard, but God is always there to help. He looked wistful. Then, remembering the restrictions in the country we were in, I said to him, "Do you know who Jesus is?" He said no and laughed, wondering I suppose why I should be asking him about someone who he presumed was a friend of mine. I then asked him again, using the name that Jesus is known by in his part of the world. Again he laughed and said no. He had absolutely no idea who I was talking about. He was no callow youth, but a married man of around twenty-eight years of age! I explained as briefly and directly as I could, just who Jesus was and why He had come to earth. I left it at that, believing that if it was right he would ask more questions when he was ready. As it happened he didn't, but was it just coincidence that two younger men were waiting outside our room on the day we left, telling us about problems they were having with their health and asking us to pray with them? You'll have to make up your own mind on that one. But before that happened we had already decided to leave the Christian album and CD player for our music-loving worker to enjoy, praying that the Lord would use it to plant many seeds in a land where it is forbidden for churches to exist.

In order to start working in the community you will probably find that you need to reorganise your life a little, so that you have the time to relate to people that you start to befriend. Also, it will probably mean that you do a little research on the foreign holiday destination to find out what level of persecution people in the country are under and what practical help you could give to them. You will be hugely blessed and become a blessing to many. But, just as any gardener would tell you, if you want the fruit, you have to do the preparation, then let the God-given sun and rain, frost and wind do their work too before the fruit finally arrives.

I end this section with wonderful news. I can say for certain that there is already someone working in your area and the place you may choose to go for your holiday, giving strength to the Christian community, helping the lonely believers originally from other cultures and faiths and labouring to see the powers of darkness pushed to one side. And that Someone is Jesus, who more and more is appearing to Muslims and others in dreams and visions in different parts of the world and revealing Himself to them as Saviour and Lord. And if that doesn't get you excited and wanting to get involved in the community, well I guess nothing will!

3. Get Informed

A further thing that you could consider doing is using the resources you have to find out what is really happening in the world. Knowledge is power! Used skilfully, the Internet is a great source of information about events in many different parts of the world. Although we live in an age of 24/7 news, I have found that the range and depth of many news programmes is quite often incomplete, with their output frequently limited by their own perspective on the subjects that they cover, the end result being that those seeking information do not get a totally unbiased account of what is really happening. I suppose that it could be argued that every news gathering organisation approaches each situation with their own stance, but it is still possible, by comparing one website with another, to get a clearer picture of what is really going on in the world than the average news programme would normally offer. For those who don't have access to the Internet I have found that the BBC's World Service seems to be a good source of general information of what is going on

around the globe, but not necessarily in Christian matters.
Some websites that Open Doors can recommend for their
reliability and depth of information are:

www.opendoorsuk.org from which you can access the
Open Doors website in your country.

http://www.state.gov/g/drl/rls/irf/2008 which is the
specific site for the very important US State
Department 2007 Report on International Religious
Freedom. This is produced annually and will always be
found via www.state.gov

www.secretbelievers.org The website dedicated to
Brother Andrew's latest book, which I have referred to
throughout this book.

www.christian.org.uk The Christian Institute is a
nondenominational Christian charity committed to
upholding the truths of the Bible.

http://www.worldevangelicals.org/commissions/rlc is
the home of the WEA Religious Liberties Commission
and they have an excellent email sign-up for regular
prayer news updates

http://www.compassdirect.org Compass Direct is a
Christian news service dedicated to providing exclusive
news, reports, interviews and analyses of situations and
events facing Christians persecuted for their faith.

http:/www.bbc.co.uk/religion/programmes/sunday/
prog_details.shtml If you want to know what religious
programmes the BBC is putting out each week, this is
the website to use.

http://www.premier.org.uk/ The Premier Radio
website, Premier Radio being a Christian Radio station
based in London, but also available to those who have
a Freeview box set for picking up digital signals for TV
and Radio programmes.

www.ucb.co.uk/radio UCB is an evangelical Christian
radio station offering a range of programmes to help
Christians in their daily lives, now available through
digital radio and to Freeview viewers.

http://www.christianitytoday.com/ The website for
Christianity Today a Christian monthly magazine,
reporting on issues both international and national
affecting the Christian church.

http://www.eauk.org/ The website for the
Evangelical Alliance which was founded in 1846 and
is the oldest alliance of evangelical Christians in the
world.

http://www.gfa.org/ Gospel for Asia. An organisation
dedicated to spreading the gospel in Asia.

http://www.joshuaproject.net/ Joshua Project is a
research initiative seeking to highlight the ethnic people
groups of the world with the least followers of Christ.

http://www.musalaha.org/ Musalaha is a non-profit
organization that seeks to promote reconciliation
between Israelis and Palestinians as demonstrated in the
life and teaching of Jesus.

http://www.jubileecampaign.co.uk/ Jubilee Campaign
is an effective human rights group bringing lasting

change to children at risk and persecuted Christian
families worldwide.

http://www.csw.org.uk/ Christian Solidarity
Worldwide is a human rights organisation which
specialises in religious freedom, works on behalf of
those persecuted for their Christian beliefs and
promotes religious liberty for all.

http://www.releaseinternational.org/ Release
International UK. An international organisation serving
the persecuted church in various ways.

✤　✤　✤

According to a report published in the Spring of 2008, Muslims
now make up about 19 percent of the world's population.
There are between 9 and 15 million Muslims living throughout Europe today and Islam has become the largest religious
minority. The Muslim birth rate in Europe is three times
higher than the non-Muslim one. If current trends continue,
the Muslim population of Europe will nearly double by 2015,
while the non-Muslim population will shrink by 3.5 percent.
　Do you feel threatened or thrilled by what you have just
read? We can choose to adopt a "bunker" mentality, wringing
our hands and hoping the future won't happen as some
predict, or we can see with eyes of faith beyond the screaming
headlines to what *God* is doing. Let me try to explain what I
mean. At one time, if Christians wanted to reach those outside
their own culture and faith they had to do so at great expense,
travelling vast distances and leaving their homeland and
friends for many years and in some cases, in previous
generations, forever. Now, in this global age, nowhere is
more than twenty-four hours away, but better still, people
groups that Christians in previous centuries had to travel vast

distances to reach have, in the last forty years or so, come to live amongst us thus making our task so much easier. All we need to do is provide suitable circumstances where we can meet them and begin to relate to them. How many do you guess might want to speak English better than they did when they first arrived in this country? How many have preconceived ideas about the society into which they have come, which will not be easily changed unless they meet people who can tell them a different story? And, for that matter, what preconceived ideas and attitudes might we need to change before engaging with them?

It stands to reason that just by spending time with them, you will be helping them improve their language skills and who knows how conversations might go when you do? But it is vital that you see them first and foremost as potential friends, rather than possible scalps to be won for your fellowship! The most powerful, beguiling and effective thing that Jesus has given Christians to work with is love. It conquers all if it is pure enough and strong enough. Take time out to remind yourself again what the Bible says about love in 1 Corinthians 13. Without it we and our message are hollow and worthless, and our faith and relationship with God turns into formal, hollow religion, which causes a stink in God's nostrils! We are living in an age where it has never been easier to obtain information – but the challenge is that one still needs to do the "spade work" in order to dig out information that is truthful and unbiased. Do you love the unreached enough to find out what is really going on in the world?

4. Get Writing

Can I also encourage you to get out your pen and paper – or your computer or laptop for that matter. Not to write critical letters or angry emails to people or organisations that you are at odds with, but supportive letters or cards giving encouragement wherever possible. I'm not talking about great screeds of wordy paragraphs here, in fact often the more precise and to the point one can be the better. We are living in the age of the email and the text message – use them to put your point over, succinctly and precisely! And for those who really can't contemplate having to write a letter no matter what device is used, well, the telephone, either landline or mobile has never been easier to employ to contact people.

Take an active part in advocacy or letter writing campaigns such as those organised by Open Doors to support persecuted Christians around the world. Further details can be found at www.opendoorsuk.org.

Having worked in television for over three years at one time in my life, I know that viewers' comments count for a lot. Each critical letter is noted, but letters of praise are highly prized! The same goes for radio. There is one radio programme that I particularly enjoyed some years ago and I wrote to the producer, asking her to thank her team for entertaining me during a stressful time in my life. Much to my surprise, some time later I received a letter from her, inviting me to visit the radio station and when I did, was treated to a tour and then afternoon tea. I was even allowed to make a very small contribution to a programme in the making on the day I visited! Now, that isn't going to happen every time a letter of praise is written, but it does indicate just how much a genuine note of encouragement is appreciated.

There is an old saying which states that the pen is mightier than the sword, so as Christians we need to learn how to use the pen skilfully to encourage those who are moving in the right direction, even if it is only to a small degree. Organisations like Amnesty International and Greenpeace are dedicated to campaigning about a range of issues using lobbying and persuasion to bring big companies and Governments around to their way of thinking. You too can play your part. Learn to network and share information with friends and church groups so they know what's going on and how to pray too. Consider investing in several copies of this book to give to people who you feel might benefit from reading these stories who would then help persecuted Christians in this country and throughout the world. It's amazing what can happen if we sow a little seed thoughtfully and prayerfully. I suppose some of the questions that need to be asked here are:

1. Who do you know who may have been or is being persecuted for being a Christian?
2. How can you help them?
3. What are the key lessons you have learnt from this book?

The main reason for Jesus coming to earth was to die on the Cross for the sins of mankind, thereby cancelling out the sin that had been brought into the world when Adam and Eve disobeyed God. But He had other tasks as well, one important one being to prepare His disciples for what would happen to them and other believers down the ages so that they would not be alarmed, but alert. Listen to what Jesus said in Luke 6:22–23:

> *"Blessed are you when men hate you,*
> *when they exclude you and insult you*
> *and reject your name as evil,*
> *because of the Son of Man.*
> *Rejoice in that day and leap for joy, because great is your reward in*
> *heaven. For that is how their fathers treated the prophets."*   (NIV)

Some who have studied this Bible passage have noticed a "progression", if I can use that word, in the attitude towards those who follow Jesus. First of all they **hate** the believer, then they **exclude**, then they **insult** and finally they **reject**. The first letters of all those words in bold make up the word **HEIR**, which reminds us of another Bible verse found in the book of Romans which says:

> *"Now if we are children, then we are heirs – heirs of God and co-heirs with Christ, if indeed we share in his sufferings in order that we may also share in his glory."*   (Romans 8:17 NIV)

It may be that you are one of those believers who have experienced the things that the verses in Luke talk of. If so, you will know that they can often leave scars of pain, frustration and depression. Maybe they still go on in your life. It could be that you have never considered the treatment you have had at the hands of others to be persecution. In the light of what you have read, what scars might you have experienced just this week? And are the things that you have had to deal with, or are still dealing with, making you stronger as a Christian, or causing your faith to fail? In either case, it might be helpful to do a little research on the subject of spiritual warfare and how it is possible to battle against spiritual forces that wage war against the Holy Spirit living in each follower of the Lord Jesus Christ. This is what the letter to the Ephesians says about spiritual warfare:

> *"For we wrestle not against flesh and blood, but against principalities, against powers, against the rulers of the darkness of this world, against spiritual wickedness in high places."*
>
> (Ephesians 6:12 KJV)

5. Get on Your Knees!

Which leads on to the next thing which should definitely be done, which is to pray for the situations that you have read about and the general spiritual climate in this country, both as an individual and, when possible, with other like-minded Christians. This could also become a real opportunity to break down the barriers that sometimes exist between Christians who only ever seem to relate to those within their own fellowship. Try meeting with Christians across your town who want to put some time aside on a regular basis to pray specifically for Christians who need encouragement and help. I'm not suggesting that people abandon life groups or prayer groups within their own fellowships, but that this be an "added extra" which could be as flexible as it needs to be. The great thing is it only needs a few phone calls to organise, can be kept small so that people can meet in a home, and doesn't involve any expenditure, apart from maybe a mug of coffee and a few chocolate biscuits – and not even that if you have decided to fast! Be sensitive to what the Holy Spirit might be revealing to you as you read your Bible and then as you pray. To pray is one of the most exciting and dynamic actions that Christians can be engaged in. Encourage an atmosphere where no one person dominates and one where the Holy Spirit has freedom to move. What a huge privilege it is to go into the presence of the Maker of the whole Universe, day or night to plead on behalf of those who suffer or who are weighed down with care. Also, prayer walking is a great way of praying constructively. Sometimes there are spiritual strongholds within an area that will yield when Christians "prayer walk" the area over a period of time.

I well remember moving to a new area of the country where local Christians were bothered by unruly behaviour from some of the local young people. The strange thing was that all the trouble-makers appeared to live in a very small area of the town, in fact most of them lived in just one street. A friend of mine and I decided to pray specifically about this problem and came to the conclusion that we should do a prayer walk in the street which housed the problem lads. I have to be honest and admit that we both felt fairly self-conscious about doing this – it was high summer and the evenings were light, so we compromised and did a "prayer drive" instead. Up and down the street we went in my friend's beaten-up old car, praying earnestly that God would deal with any spiritual forces for evil that might be over the street and affecting the behaviour of its young people. After a while we felt we had done all that we could do and went home. There was no immediate change in the situation as far as we could tell, but about ten days later we happened to hear that the local vicar had had some new visitors to his youth club. The five or six lads that turned up did so because of the persuasion of their gang member who had been the chief trouble maker in the village – who "just happened" to live in the street we had prayed in. A few weeks later he gave his heart to the Lord and then, because he was a natural leader, influenced a lot of his peers. Prayer walking (or prayer driving if you are a wimp like me) is definitely worth considering.

6. Get Praising the Lord

Finally, the thing to do probably most of all is to give thanks! I became terribly burdened for the people that I interviewed whilst writing this book, those whose stories have made it into print and all the others that didn't for one reason or another. Often I was the first person that they had told their full story to and I carried the weight of that responsibility with me for many months, feeling troubled for their welfare and ongoing walk with the Lord. In the end it started to be a bigger burden for me than it should have been. I realised that I wasn't doing what I should have done, which was to take all their situations to the Lord. I should have reminded myself of the advice that Peter gives in 1 Peter 5:7:

> *"Cast all your anxiety on him because he cares for you."*   (NIV)

What I needed was someone to remind me that the battle is His! They are *His* children, it's *His* work and *He* is in control! It's good to be concerned, but it's important also to give our burdens and the burdens that we carry for others to God. A very positive way of praying, rather than constantly asking God to do this or that, is to thank Him in advance for all that He is doing and will do in the future! There is power in praise and I know God wants us all to be a praising people. He will build His Church, He knows how to direct and guide and provide. We have an amazing God who sent His Son to die so that we can be in total union with Him. Praise, I believe, is a very powerful way of confronting spiritual strongholds, because it allows us to focus on all that God is doing, rather than the mischief that the enemy has caused. Have you read Psalm 150 recently? What a praise session the psalmist was suggesting! This is just one of the Psalms and indeed other parts of Scripture where the importance of praise is emphasised.

It could be, of course, that far from being surprised about what you have read in this book, you are someone who has suffered persecution because of the Christian values you hold and the life that you live. You too might have come from a Muslim background, or be someone who has experienced the heavy hand of officialdom when you have tried to express your Christian faith in the community. You may be having a tough time with school mates or work colleagues or even another member of your family if you have found Jesus as Saviour and they are still on the journey of faith. If you are in any of those categories you might be wondering what, if anything, there is that you can do to get support or advice. James, who was a brother of Jesus, wrote this as encouragement to the church down the ages:

> *"Consider it pure joy, my brothers, whenever you face trials of many kinds, because you know that the testing of your faith develops perseverance. Perseverance must finish its work so that you may be mature and complete, not lacking anything."*
>
> (James 1:2–4 NIV)

That is a hard thing to read, especially when you are in the midst of difficulties, but there is so much truth in those verses which make us strong in times of trial. However, often in those kinds of times the value of speaking to an understanding individual who could give you practical help and advice is inestimable. If that is your situation right now, can I suggest that you contact Open Doors, an organisation that has been supporting Christians under persecution for over fifty years. They have many resources to hand, some of which have been mentioned already, and even if they were not able to give you the particular support and encouragement that you need, they would do their best to put you in touch with others in your area who could. Here is a list of the websites that you can use to get in touch with an Open Doors office, depending on which country you are living in, starting with the international website:

International Website: www.od.org
Australia: www.opendoors.org.au
Brazil: www.portasabertas.org.br
Canada: www.opendoorsca.org
Denmark: www.forfulgt.dk
France: www.portesouvertes.fr
Germany: www.opendoors-de.org
Italy: www.porteaperteitalia.org
Korea: www.opendoors.or.kr
The Netherlands: www.opendoors.nl
New Zealand: www.opendoors.org.nz
Norway: www.opendoors.no
Philippines: http://ph.od.org/index.php
Singapore: www.opendoors.org/ODS/
South Africa: www.opendoors.org.za
Spain: www.puertasabiertas.org/
Switzerland (French): www.portesouvertes.ch
Switzerland (German): www.opendoors.ch
UK and Ireland: www.opendoorsuk.org
USA: www.odusa.org

Persecution can often make people feel isolated and afraid. If
you are someone who is currently facing persecution because
of your Christian beliefs I want you to know that you are
not alone. Open Doors estimates that there are more than
100 million Christians who are facing persecution for their
faith in Jesus Christ. But for those of us who are not
persecuted, what should our attitude to our persecuted
brethren be? The parable of the good Samaritan as told in
the Gospel of Luke 10:30–36 gives us a clue. We must never
lose sight of the fact that Jesus said that the Church was His
body and as Paul reminds us in his letter to the Corinthians, if
one part of the body suffers, we all suffer. Maybe we need to
reflect on the fact that what is happening to one part of the
body today, could be the fate of another still protected part of
the body tomorrow! No one wants to think about persecution
or being attacked for our faith, but just for a moment, ask
yourself this: if you were harassed for your faith, what would
your reaction be? Would you seek revenge or offer forgiveness instead? One way makes the problem worse and is the
way of the world. The other is the King's High Way and opens
a door of opportunity and hope.

The Bible encourages us to, *"Buy the truth and do not sell it"*
(Proverbs 23:23 NIV) and getting the truth is harder and harder
to obtain, even in our own society. If you attend a church
which regularly preaches from the Bible and consistently gives
out a Gospel message, you are in a minority. The sands of the
desert are doing their work. We are in a spiritual battle, but
less and less people, even in the Church, recognise and
understand what is going on. But if you are one of those
who is convinced that we are engaged in a spiritual war,
should you not commit to a life of prayer? Soldiers in a war
zone are totally committed, even to the point of laying down
their lives for their country. Should we not consider even that
possibility for the Kingdom of God? How much do you value
the eternal life that you have been given? Should you be called

to do so, would you consider giving up your natural life here on earth in order that someone else, maybe many more, could hear, understand and accept God's eternal life? As I once heard Brother Andrew say, Jesus' command to His disciples was to go into all the world and preach the Gospel – but He never said anything about coming back again!

In the Gospel of Luke, Jesus tells His disciples that the harvest is truly great, but the labourers are few. Although the freedoms that the Christian Church in the West has are being eroded, we still have freedoms that other parts of the Church can only dream of. We need to wake up, know and believe the Bible, and do the things that Jesus told us to do before the end of the age arrives. It is at this stage important again to mention spiritual warfare and to look into what it means to battle against spiritual forces through prayer, fasting and using the Word of God (which is described as the Sword of the Spirit), with skill and precision. This is what the book of Ephesians has to say about it:

> *"Finally, be strong in the Lord and in his mighty power. Put on the full armour of God so that you can take your stand against the devil's schemes. For our struggle is not against flesh and blood, but against the rulers, against the authorities, against the powers of this dark world and against the spiritual forces of evil in the heavenly realms. Therefore put on the full armour of God, so that when the day of evil comes, you may be able to stand your ground, and after you have done everything, to stand. Stand firm then, with the belt of truth buckled round your waist, with the breastplate of righteousness in place, and with your feet fitted with the readiness that comes from the gospel of peace. In addition to all this, take up the shield of faith, with which you can extinguish all the flaming arrows of the evil one. Take the helmet of salvation and the sword of the Spirit, which is the word of God. And pray in the Spirit on all occasions with all kinds of prayers and requests. With this in mind, be alert and always keep on praying for all the saints."*   (Ephesians 6:10–18 NIV)

It is so easy to get disturbed or confused or discouraged by all that is going on in the world. When that happens we need to remember the words of Jesus who told His followers that in the world they would have tribulation, but to be of good cheer, because He has overcome the world (John 16:33). May you be blessed as you work and pray and give to God, so that one day the God of all creation will be able to say to you, "Well done!"

Summary

Having read this book, you might have been left thinking hard about the whole subject of persecution of Christians. Maybe up until now you thought you had a fairly clear idea in your mind what the persecution of Christians was all about. Perhaps you thought of it as the denial of education to a child whose parents are living in a Communist country, or the lack of job promotion for an adult living under a religious regime opposed to Christianity. Or perhaps when you heard the word "persecution" your thoughts would immediately go to people languishing in prisons because they had been caught reading the Bible or had been discovered teaching biblical truths to minors. All these things and things of a much more serious nature still go on, on a regular basis, in different parts of the world. And if you wish to know more about these kind of situations, you can read the excellent book entitled *Faith That Endures* which has been written by Ronald Boyd-MacMillan and recently published by Revell with a foreword by Brother Andrew, that tells in much more detail than I can go into here just what is happening in various parts of the world to followers of the Lord Jesus Christ.

But now you have read *this* book I hope it has begun to make you aware of a kind of persecution that is often much more subtle and insidious, but equally as damaging and restrictive to those who have experienced it, which is happening to Christians in the United Kingdom **today**.

For those mentioned in the pages of this book, the question "Could persecution come here?" has been answered already. Restrictions on street preaching, restrictions on what can be said in the pulpit, ridicule in the classroom and workplace, intimidation and death threats are some of the situations that people like you and I are having to deal with, just because they follow Jesus and have refused to compromise their faith. But as is the case in most countries, it is difficult to make a general statement about persecution which applies to the whole of the United Kingdom. Restrictions that various local councils have brought into being in some parts of the country might be unknown in other parts. What would not be allowed to be said in some pulpits would be welcomed in others. There is not a lot that is uniform throughout the whole country, except perhaps the attitude of non-Christian faith groups to those within their community who convert to Christianity. However, next time you read one of the letters in the New Testament, telling as they do the pressures that the still young Church was under, let it act as a reminder to you to pray for those who are experiencing pressure because of their faith in Jesus today, maybe in the town where you live. And if you are one of those believers who are suffering in this way, let it be an encouragement to you and a reminder that in those times, as now, God was aware of all that was happening and was able to use their circumstances to strengthen the faith of the Church and to spread its message of salvation.

It would be reasonable to assume that the problems that Christians face in Muslim countries would be very different from the difficulties that believers in the West have to deal with. But contrast the recent book written by Brother Andrew and Al Janssen – *Secret Believers* (published by Hodder and Stoughton, ISBN 978-0340863-06-0). This tells the story of Christians in an un-named Muslim country and one can easily see how similar the problems can be for Christians in the West as well as the non-Christian world. For instance, this book tells of the trials of Fred Hammond and his church members who struggled with Muslims that wanted Fred and his fellow church members out of the area. In Andrew's book we read of Father Alexander who is constantly intimidated and hampered from carrying out his duties as a priest. This book has told the story of Lela, forced into marriage at a very young age – the same thing happened to Layla in the Brother Andrew book. Pressure was put upon Trevor to compromise his faith in the chapter entitled "Festival to a Foreign God" and in Andrew's book Salima was forced to compromise her faith, almost before she was a believing Christian! It is shocking to think that threats can be made on a person's life because of their religious beliefs, but that is what happened to Shirlee in this book, and to Ahmed in *Secret Believers*.

However, not all the similarities are because of the terrible things that people are experiencing. For instance, in this book we read how Jesus appeared to Lela at a very difficult point in her life and in *Secret Believers* we discover how Jesus also personally appeared to Mustafa.

Someone once said that bad things happen when good people fail to act. If we look back at history we can see that the religious freedom we have had in this country was hard fought for. People were burnt at the stake for the beliefs they held or for translating the Bible into the English language. They cared more about the truths that had been revealed to them than their own personal safety. There are still some people like that in our country today. But it is sad to reflect that many true believers have been lulled into a place of false security. Because there has been religious freedom in this country for so long, they think that it will continue forever. But tides are turning and attitudes are changing towards Christians and the message they bring. Because of our multi-cultural society, together with political correctness, it is increasingly difficult to say anything of a definitive nature. It is more and more the case that everything now has to be of an all-inclusive nature so as not to offend anyone. And although religious minorities should have the right to practise their own religion, Christians must never lose *their* right to be able to say, legally and without any cultural, social or religious barriers being imposed upon them, what they truly believe, which is that Jesus Christ is the only way to God. Any lesser statement is a watering down of the truth and leads people on a false road with false hope at the end of it.

Christianity, real Christianity, has always been controversial and dangerous. That is because, if taken seriously, it contains the most incredible life-changing message, the impact of which goes on throughout eternity. It is one that tyrants and governments have feared throughout history, because they recognise its power. Sadly, a large part of the Christian Church in the UK today appears to be slumbering, not bothering to get involved in preaching the Gospel message, whilst at the same time allowing itself to be entertained by those who use the Christian Gospel for their own ends.

Open Doors has produced some very exciting and informative resources for use within churches and house groups, including films, prayer materials, audio CDs and books such as this one and the one mentioned earlier called *Faith That Endures*, which are designed to alert the Church to what is happening in our country right now and perhaps even more importantly what they need to do to prepare themselves for the potentially difficult days that lie ahead.

Brother Andrew once said that he had only ever heard two statements made by Christian leaders regarding persecution. The first one was: *Persecution will never happen here*. The second one was: *I never **thought** persecution would ever happen here*. The fact is that as we come closer to the return to earth of Jesus for His church, we *will* see persecution. I believe that it is inevitable. But there are ways in which we as Christians can be prepared for what is to come, learning from the experiences of believers in other lands that have gone through this and adapting some of what they have learnt to fit the situation here in our own country.

So, far from being doom laden, this book carries a message of hope. God has forewarned us as to what we can expect and He expects us to use the resources that He has given us to strengthen and equip ourselves and every other member of His Church.

I trust that after coming to the end of this book you will want to pray for those that you have read about, seek out the Open Doors materials that I have mentioned, and prepare yourself spiritually for what lies ahead. And may God richly bless you as you continue in The Way.

David Waite
October 2008

Epilogue

This book is a challenge. It is a challenge to understanding and a challenge to commitment and action. It is a challenge to individuals and churches to live as authentic disciples of Jesus Christ.

Open Doors has been part of that challenge and part of the response for more than fifty years. It started in 1955 with a Dutch missionary discovering that Christians in Communist countries were desperately longing for supplies of the Bible – and so he took a suitcase full of Christian literature behind the Iron Curtain. He became known as Brother Andrew – "God's Smuggler".

Fifty years later Open Doors is supporting persecuted Christians in over fifty countries. This book has given a small insight into its work in Muslim countries; similar work is supported in Africa, Asia and Latin America, whether the oppression comes in the name of communism, Buddhism, Hinduism or Islam. Where the people of God are under pressure, Open Doors stands with them, responding to their cries for help and shaping its response under their guidance.

Right now Open Doors is ready to give you information for your prayers – the authentic voice of the Persecuted Church brought to you in print, by email, on the web, so that your prayers are timely, informed and effective weapons in the spiritual battle.

Right now Open Doors can channel your gifts to where they will make a significant difference to our sisters and brothers in the Persecuted Church. Providing the Bibles and other Christian literature they have requested; supporting the training of pastors and congregations so that they can stand strong through the storm; strengthening the Church in its commitment to mission, so that even under pressure it can reach out with the Gospel of Jesus Christ; enabling those who have lost so much to receive practical help and spiritual encouragement.

Right now Open Doors is enabling many Christians around the world to build personal relationships with the Persecuted Church as they travel to share encouragement, to pray, to bring Bibles and other literature. And many also volunteer to bring the Persecuted Church into the life of their own church family, sharing news for prayer and exploring the lessons to be learned from our sisters and brothers.

Getting involved with Open Doors is not the complete or only answer to meeting the challenges posed by this book, but it is a great start! Open Doors is committed to encouraging and supporting you as you respond – by linking you to your persecuted family around the world, so that you can pray with them and not just for them; so that you can learn from them as well as give to them; so that, together, we can all play our part in God's great plan and purpose for His world.

It would be a privilege to be part of your response to *A Time to Speak*. For further information, simply contact the Open Doors office in your area via the websites listed a few pages earlier.

And may you know God's blessing as you follow Him in faithful obedience and radical commitment.

> "Our very mission is called 'Open Doors' because we believe that any door is open, any time and anywhere . . . to proclaim Christ."
> (Brother Andrew)

We hope you enjoyed reading this New Wine book.
For details of other New Wine books
and a wide range of titles from other
Word and Spirit publishers visit our website:
www.newwineministries.co.uk
email: newwine@xalt.co.uk